M000307404

YOUR HIDDEN SEASON

DISCOVERING THE
BEAUTY IN THE WAIT

BY

LISA DANNIELLE

Copyright © 2019 by Lisa Dannielle

All rights reserved. No part of this publication may be reproduced, distributed, or transmitted in any form or by any means, including photocopying, recording, or other electronic or mechanical methods, without the prior written permission of the publisher, except in the case of brief quotations embodied in critical reviews and certain other noncommercial uses permitted by copyright law. For permission requests, write to the publisher, addressed "Attention: Permissions Coordinator," at the address below.

Brielle Book Publishers
539 W. Commerce #525
Dallas, TX 75208
Ph: 972-638-7287

Ordering Information:
Quantity sales. Special discounts are available on quantity purchases by corporations, associations, and others. For details, contact the publisher at the address above.

Printed in the United States of America

Paperback: 978-1-7335201-0-2
Hardback: 978-1-7335201-1-9
Ebook: 978-1-7335201-2-6

First Edition

BRIELLE BOOK
PUBLISHERS

"Anticipation is the feeling of hopeful expectation, believing in the magic of what has been and what might be again. This we know to be true: There is wonder in waiting..."

-Joanna Gaines

DEDICATION

To the dreamers, the forgotten ones....

You are a work of art!

TABLE OF CONTENTS

FOREWORD

As you read *"Your Hidden Season, Discovering the Beauty in the Wait"* you will experience joy, laughter and total amusement. From the same pages you will experience pain, sadness and heartache. However, interwoven through the raw, real and extremely transparent story of Lisa Dannielle you will realize that someone understands exactly how you feel. You will be comforted by the fact, that someone has gone through the same thing you have. You will be encouraged in knowing, that you are not the only one who is hidden. You will begin to believe, that there is a greater purpose for all of the madness that you are facing in your life.

Sometimes, all you need to make it through the challenges that you are facing in your life, is knowing that someone else has been there and done that and is still alive to tell about it. Lisa is not just alive to tell about it, she is using her story to help others. She gives you some incredible insight on how to process the pain of "waiting" for your dream to be realized and finding the beauty in the middle of the process. Oftentimes, it is then, in the waiting, that God shows you, that what He wanted all along, was YOU. The "waiting," was God's way of getting your attention, so He could have a deeper, richer, fuller and more intimate relationship with you. It is only then, in the proper healthy relationship with our wonderful Savior, Jesus Christ, are we able to realize the beautiful plan that God has for our lives.

So, get ready to laugh and cry as you read through the pages of *"Your Hidden Season, Discovering the Beauty in the Wait."* But more importantly get ready to see yourself, your circumstances and others, differently than you ever have before. You will never feel "hidden" again.

Pastor Kendall Bridges
Lead Pastor, Freedom Church
Author of ***"Better Marriage, Against All Odds"***

INTRODUCTION

Hello, my lovelies! I am so excited to share this book with you, and to be completely transparent, I fought tooth and nail with this book. When God placed it on my heart, I had no idea why He told me, of all people, to write it. You see, I am no angel. I am not perfect by any stretch of the imagination. God seriously could not have chosen a more flawed person to deliver this message. I have been through bad relationships, a failed marriage, adultery, domestic violence, and low self-worth. If it was bad and forced you to your knees, I probably went through it, all while being a "church girl." You heard me right—I was a church girl, and probably the worst type of church girl at that. I was in church every Sunday and sometimes up to three times a week, and I was still… broken.

Now I am one of those people who can truly say that my deliverance was a miracle. I do not say that to be dramatic; I say it because I still marvel at God's faithfulness and how He is willing to use a broken vessel to unleash freedom in other women. I marvel at how He can see you in your worst state, clean you up, love you completely, and still want you to step out for His glory.

This book was a battle. When it began, it was a comedic singles' self-help book that highlighted some misadventures I had in dating and how to be content as a single woman since that is what I finally was. I thought it would be funny and relevant, but it turns out that isn't what God wanted to discuss after all. As I was going through the writing process, this book began to evolve—and I did, too. As I looked back at the situations I had faced in my life, I realized that a great deal of the successes that I had found in those paralyzing situations were a direct result of my intentional pursuit of God. As I sought to understand Him and see Him more clearly, I realized that this book was much less about how NOT to be single and was much more about learning to see myself clearly in my season of singleness.

God really impressed upon me that this book and this life is not about me and another man. It is about Him and me. My relationship with my heavenly Father, who loves me and who gives good gifts. It is about a pursuit to know Him in such a way that I can see Him in every situation. This sight, this understanding, suddenly makes me aware of only what He wants for me, and in that place of understanding, I can truly say I only desire what He wants for me—even if it means I have to wait longer to get it. As a single person, in all things, our desire should be to have what God wants to get to us, not what He wants to keep away from us.

This book took some bravery. Think about it. We all want to tell the wonderful truths of what God has done for us, but we want to abbreviate it. We like talking about the victory, but very few want to discuss the discouraging, muddy, and downright ugly path that some of us had to take to get there. No offense, but I certainly did not want you all up in my business. Conversely, nothing in this book is something that I have the right to hide. God has not only completely changed my life, but He has completely revolutionized the way I see Him and His people. He has taken every hurt, and He has healed me in a way that has astounded even myself.

I was a mess. After my journey, I just could not fathom that there was anything left of me for Him to use. But in true God form, He takes these messes that we create of our own lives and makes something more beautiful than we could ever imagine, and I am no different. Yes, I was messed up. Yes, I had issues. Some issues existed far before I even met a man. I was completely in the dark, walking around every day, oblivious to how those issues were setting the tone for every decision I would make in my adult life. I had no idea how my faulty thinking was keeping me from the best God had planned for me and leaving me with mere… options. Options are not a good thing when none of them are God's best. Nevertheless, in an attempt to be faithful to God, I am writing this book. I am no critically acclaimed relationship expert—actually, I'm quite the opposite. I am merely someone who cares.

A friend of mine, an amazing author in her own right, and I were talking one day, and I told her how I toiled with the notion of telling my story. She said that only the truth sets people free. She then expressed regret about not being completely transparent in her own book and said, "Lisa, you just have to tell it!" I thank God for her and her heart for me. God definitely knows who and what you need in the moment that you need it.

So, in this book, we will take a journey together. We will talk about relationships, singleness, triumphs, and failures. I want to be real with you, with no sugarcoating and just the honest truth. Allow me to reiterate that this is not a book about how you can get a man. Getting a man is easy! Ha ha, I feel like I heard twenty of you yell, "No it isn't!" But I will say it again— getting *a* man is easy! Getting *the* man is hard!

In the twenty-first century, waiting to be found by someone who is running hard after God is a challenge! This is primarily because there are many men in all realms and some in the church that look the part but may not be living in a way that pleases God. Either way, this is not a how-to-get-your-man book! But don't be discouraged! We will talk about men at length. Just remember, my love, that men are not the primary focus of this book—*you* are. You, with your beautiful self, are the goal! The Word of God says, "But seek ye first the kingdom of God, and his righteousness; and all these things shall be added unto you" (Matthew 6:33, KJV). Yes, ladies, this includes men. God wants to be first. No! He *has* to be first!

So, we are going to discuss our lives and our priorities, and then as we get our ducks in a row, the men will come. I promise!

My heart's desire is that you can find release in these words. Because if you can, I promise by the power of the risen Savior that your life will never be the same. We will talk about God's will for our lives, and we will dive into what we are feeling and what may be missing. I promise by the end of this book, you will see yourself through a clearer lens and have confidence that God is not far off. In fact, He is close to you. He loves you and is so meticulous about your heart that He sees fit to hide you. Yes, He sees you and He knows you but, even better, He remembers you. You are hidden but not forgotten.

Let's Pray

Heavenly Father, as we embark on this journey together, I first want to thank You for all of the beautiful women that will read this book. Thank You for hearing them, for knowing them, and even more for remembering them. God, I ask that You bless them with grace for the journey. I ask that You reveal Yourself to them in this season and also that You would encourage them as they walk in this world as the exalted women You have called them to be. I pray You will lift their heads and grant them courage in their pursuit of You.

Lord, make my words resonate with their spirits, and I ask that You plant the seeds that need to be planted and discard what needs to be discarded. Awaken us, oh God. Show us who we are, show us who we can become and, more importantly, show us who YOU are. Expose the faulty thinking that we have developed as a result of living in this world. Strengthen, protect, heal, deliver, save, and set free. You are our hearts' desire, and we thank You for all these gifts in your Son Jesus's name. Amen.

CHAPTER 1

YOU'RE HIDDEN

—～～—

> *For in the time of trouble he shall hide me in his*
> *pavilion: in the secret of his tabernacle shall he hide*
> *me; he shall set me up upon a rock.*
>
> ### *Psalm 27:5 KJV*

What Does It Mean to Be Hidden?

Have you ever felt like you were invisible? There is something to be said about feeling like no one sees you. Think about it with me for a minute. There was a season in your life when men were beating down the door. I mean, you could not go anywhere without a couple of men approaching you, and now it seems like you can have on your Sunday best and no one even knows you are alive. Or maybe you are constantly bombarded with attention from the opposite sex, yet not one of them is: a) who you want; or b) who you need.

Why is that? Is it because you are less beautiful than you were before? No. Is it because you have suddenly become uninteresting? No. Is it because all men are intimidated by your independence or financial status? No again. You look at yourself and you are better than ever, more beautiful than you have ever been, and you're still... single. You instantly start questioning yourself: *What is going on? Where is this beautiful man of purpose I thought I would meet? Why is everyone signing the dotted line on their happily-ever-after, and I am still over here hashtagging #relationshipgoals? What is happening?*

If any of this sounds remotely like you, then I want to take a moment to encourage you. Perhaps this state you are in has nothing to do with you. It's not your beauty, or your lack thereof, and it isn't your financial status. Yes, you are still exciting. You may even be the life of the party—you may just be hidden.

According to the *Merriam-Webster* dictionary, "hidden" means "kept out of sight or concealed." Isn't that something? In the Word of God, we always see God taking His people to a place of seclusion to advance them in whatever their given task was, but surely He is not still secluding His people. Or is He?

If you suddenly find yourself in a place of seclusion, then you are in great company. Some of the most memorable people in the Bible were secluded before God took them to their next level. When we hear about these stories, we always seem to remember the result and diminish the struggle. In scripture, these people weren't destitute before God called them. They had money, family, and sometimes fame when God called them to a place of silence. Think about that for a minute—their lives were good!

Moses was a prince before he was driven out into the wilderness to ultimately save a people he didn't even know. Joseph was his father's favorite before he was sold into slavery, and Paul had some notoriety for being a persecutor of Christians. For all intents and purposes, these men had no reason to volunteer for service to God. Yet, God pulled them from everything they thought they knew to be normal and hid them away for His use. Even the great prophet Elijah was pulled away to seclusion. Elijah! It is not like he was oblivious to who God was; he didn't need convincing or reminding of God's sovereignty. Elijah was on the battlefield, preaching and prophesying, and God still decided that He needed him to Himself for a period of time.

That's hard! You mean to tell me, it is entirely possible to be moving in the things of God and still be required to drop everything to pursue Him on a deeper level? The short answer is yes. Sometimes seclusion is necessary so that we are aware of the next stage in the journey. Don't believe me? Let's look at the Word of God:

"Then the word of the Lord came to Elijah: 'Leave here, turn eastward and hide in the Kerith Ravine, east of the Jordan. You will drink from the brook, and I have directed the ravens to supply you with food there'" (1 Kings 17:2–6, NIV). So Elijah did what the Lord had told him. He went to the Kerith Ravine, east of the Jordan, and stayed there. The ravens brought him bread and meat in the morning and bread and meat in the evening, and he drank from the brook.

I just couldn't understand it—why does God pull us away? He is God. It certainly isn't because He needs something from us; He can do anything at the snap of His fingers. Even the Word of God says the cattle on a thousand hills belongs to Him, so why bring us to a place of solitude with Him? Consider for a moment that it is not to get something *from* us, but to pour something *into* us. God will sometimes pull you away from everything you think you know so that He can do in you what needs to be done to equip you for the journey.

In a moment of transparency, I remember when I truly surrendered my life to the Lord. I had been serving Him for over thirty years but had never asked for a personal relationship with Him. When I finally said, "Yes, I will do whatever You want me to do," He revealed the calling on my life and immediately pulled me away from everything I thought I knew. Unbeknownst to me, God required me to enter a desert place. A place for just Him and me, so we could develop our relationship. I wish I could say that I went willingly, but I didn't. I fought to hold on to the previous life I thought I had, but it wasn't God's desire for me anymore. He needed to move me, and I needed to be okay with it.

You see, when God moves you, it usually begins with a mental move. He elevates your thinking so that you can begin to understand His ways, then He moves you emotionally and you can feel His presence. And sometimes He moves you physically from among those you know to a strange land where you have to lean wholly and completely on Him to navigate your way in your new surroundings. This may happen in any order, but the bottom line is: get ready to move.

God has need of you. For whatever reason, God has chosen to keep you out of sight. So embrace it; don't fight it. Trust me, fighting it only makes it longer and more tedious. If God has chosen you for a season of seclusion, it does not matter who you try to put in your life; if He does not want them there, it will not work. This applies to friends, family, and love relationships. If it is not for His purpose, it will not happen.

This is the season in your life that God has chosen to "make" you. Jeremiah 18:3–6 (MSG) says, "So I went to the potter's house, and sure enough, the potter was there, working away at his wheel. Whenever the pot that the potter was working on turned out badly, as sometimes happens when you are working with clay, the potter would simply start over and use the same clay to make another pot. Then God's Message came to me: 'Can't I do just as this potter does, people of Israel?' God's Decree! 'Watch this potter. In the same way that this potter works his clay, I work on you, people of Israel.'"

To be in a hidden season with God is to essentially be on the potter's wheel. If you have grown up in church, then you have heard of some references to the potter. I thought I was fairly familiar with the pottery process, and from what I knew, the process wasn't very fun. But in preparation of writing this book, I researched a little further and saw this scripture in a totally different way.

Let's take a look, shall we? First, every kind of clay isn't ideal for everything. There are different clays for different purposes, and isn't this true for the body of Christ as well? I watched a documentary that showed the process that Native Americans went through to make some of the historic pottery that grace some of the iconic museums we frequent today. When you examine it closely, the process is pretty remarkable.

These talented women began with an ugly mud-like substance, which they molded and spun into beautiful vessels. I remember watching in wonder and just marveling at the fact that these women could be so artistic, and every now and then, just when I thought these jars of clay were at their finishing stage, the potter would surprise me. She would see a small imperfection or blemish that seemed miniscule and insignificant, and she would destroy the entire vessel to begin again.

Imagine how frustrating that had to be for her. When asked why she had to start over instead of just patching over the area, she explained that the blemish would have compromised the integrity of the entire vessel. You see, there are more difficult stages that this vessel will have to survive. So, the clay pot has to be perfect before it goes into the fire to be finished. Did you hear what I said? It has to be complete BEFORE the fire!

We all have unique gifts and talents for God to cultivate in us, but He has to make us pliable, and that requires a process. When a potter begins the process, he has to determine the function of the vessel, and once he realizes what he wants the vessel to become, he chooses the clay. As mentioned, some clays are stronger than others. He knows this going in, so he throws this clay on the table and begins to work. In fact, "throwing" is the actual term that potters use when molding the clay. When he is throwing the clay, he never forgets its purpose, and he has everything the clay needs near the wheel. In the process, the potter may notice slight imperfections, and he may allow them to remain because of the character that it adds to the vessel. But sometimes there are defects in the clay that require a complete crushing of the vessel, so the potter can begin again.

In a different pottery documentary, the interviewer questioned this potter on his seemingly obsessive-compulsive behavior. She seemed quite annoyed that he kept starting over and over on this one particular piece he was working on. Finally, after he had destroyed yet another piece of his handiwork, she said to him, "Why did you do that? It looked fine to me—you must be a perfectionist." He laughed and replied, "Yes, I am a perfectionist, but I know what I am looking for!"

God is the same way in molding us. He knows what purpose He desires to bring out of us. What good is it for us to be devastatingly beautiful and so flawed that we can't carry out His purpose? It is a tragedy to only be beautiful. What else do you have? What do you have inside you that God is molding away so that you can become the vessel He needs you to be, inside and out? This is why He brings you to a place of seclusion—He intends to mold you into the most beautiful vessel this world has ever seen, but your imperfections and your calling are no one's business. He needs to get you alone, so you can be made into what He wants you to be.

The good news is that Jesus, the master potter, can start His creation from nothing. I am sure by now you have an idea of how frustrating this process can be, and if any of it resonates with you, then you, my dear, know what it is to be hidden. You see, to be hidden is to be molded on the potter's wheel. Chances are that you are in your hidden years, and you don't even realize that is where you are. You may think it is a season where no one sees your talents or hears your voice. You may think you are in a storm and no one sees you struggling. You are waiting and frustrated! Some of you may even be so focused on the destination that you are unaware of where you currently stand with your walk with God.

To be hidden is to completely surrender to God, and once that happens, He takes you to a place where you can be made whole. When you get to the end of yourself and you declare that you do not want anything but what God wants for you, He takes you to a special place where only you and He reside. Don't be discouraged that you are not "seen" right now. Embrace God choosing you for this season. Embrace what He is doing in you and ask Him to show you what He is changing. Remember that you are His child; you are His favorite. We all are. We all have the awesome opportunity to have a unique relationship with Him.

As this book goes to print, I am forty-two years old. Forty-two and still waiting for God's promise. Isn't God funny that way? He asks you if you trust Him, and the moment that you say yes, He gives you an opportunity to display it. I am no different. I was lamenting with God and asking Him what He desired for me. If I am honest with you, initially I was asking God for what I desired for me. I had no idea at the time that what He wanted was for me to go through a process in order to know Him better. Little did I know at that time, it would be knowing Him that would change everything.

Picture this: here I am, crying before the Lord, telling Him all of the reasons that life was so hard for me and in the same breath asking Him to send me someone who would love me completely. I mean, I was going for it in my prayer time. You know those sweating prayers! I was decreeing, declaring, preaching, speaking in tongues—you name it, I did it. I believe God was listening to me, but what I was seeing was not matching what I was petitioning God for.

Finally, I said the hardest words I ever had to utter in my life. Are you ready? I said, "God, whatever You want for my life, I will wait for You." You would think that it was some grand revelation—and it only took me my entire life to get there—but it was music to God's ears, and He answered me immediately. There was no loud celestial declaration, just a still, small voice: "Lisa, you are not ready." It was like taking a bullet! What do you mean I am not ready? I immediately began to plead my case. Do you know what I have been through? I began spouting off all of the sacrifices I'd made, and I think at some point I actually yelled, "And I am not having sex! Really?"

Have you ever talked to God like He wasn't God? Like He was on vacation while you went through the roughest seasons of your life? Well, needless to say, I was mortified. I could not believe that after all of my years of waiting, this would be my answer from the Lord. I was, well, in a word, angry. I felt like it was unfair. I mean, here I was, genuinely trying to live a life before Him that was holy. I had cut off everyone who was not beneficial to my walk. I stopped entertaining texts from people who did not need to be in my life. I relocated, changed my life, and dedicated time to just Him and me, And still, I wasn't ready?

If you have ever been in this difficult place with God, I want you to know you are not alone. God does things differently! Sometimes you can be doing everything completely the right way but not receive what you want right away. Remember this: God making you wait does not always mean you are outside the will of God. You do not know what God has in store; we are all on the potter's wheel. You may have made extreme progress. You may even be able to identify areas where you know God has advanced you, and while you are going through all of that molding, remember that we all still have to be tried in the fire.

Romans 8:18 (KJV) says, "For I reckon that the sufferings of this present time are not worthy to be compared with the glory which shall be revealed in us." Take it from me, the molding never ends—it just gets you perfected for the season you are in. But as you continue to live for Him, you will notice that God will begin to reveal other issues He wants to resolve, and then He begins the breaking and molding in another area of your life. It is a frustrating and sometimes confusing process, but it is well worth it. I am sure if you look back on some of your areas of deliverance, you can identify some behaviors that you will never return to.

When God has you tucked away from the rest of the world, He will begin to speak with you and abide with you in ways you never imagined. It can be so exhilarating and perhaps even a little frustrating in the beginning. When the Holy Spirit begins to converse with you on an intimate level, He is going to tell you everything that grieves Him. It was the weirdest thing for me to adjust to because I immediately became aware of things that I never thought bothered God that for **me** was sin. I can hear some of you pulling out the Ten Commandments and saying there is no truth to there being sin that only applies to individuals but let me qualify that with scripture. James 4:17 (NIV) says, "If anyone, then, knows the good they ought to do and doesn't do it, it is sin for them."

In my youth, my mother used to reference a common passage of scripture that used to frustrate me to no end. She would quote from Luke 12:48 (AMPC): "'For everyone to whom much is given, of him shall much be required; and of him to whom men entrust much, they will require and demand all the more.'" I hated it! I never understood why I was always the one that had to do things the right way. Everyone else could live their lives with no concern for God at all and still prosper, but when it was me? Oh, I had to toe the line! I could be doing everything in my power to obey, but if I decided that I would have a hogpen moment, God unleashed on me like never before.

It seemed so unfair… I loved God, and I was human, too. I have desires and dreams like everyone else and, yes, I even have my days when I don't want to emulate Christ. So why can some laugh in God's face and receive everything they want, and I have to wait? I mean, at least I am trying, right? Boy, when we are rationalizing our sins, we can come up with a million arguments for our behavior, can't we? I even had a list of people I felt deserved to wait instead of me. But God loves His children enough to chastise them. He won't allow us to stay the same, and He won't allow us to deflect the attention from our own lives. Life with Him requires evolution and growth, and you can't do that without taking responsibility for your own behavior.

Just like a father, He simply listened to me, professed His undying love for me through His Word, and then explained His reasoning. Very clearly, He said, "If I give you a blessing before you are ready, there are only two possible outcomes: 1) you will destroy it; or 2) it will destroy you." Please bear in my mind that this applies to any blessing you ask God for, not just a spouse! He continued: "I have to process you so that your character will display the responsibility necessary for the giftings on your life—gifts that have lay dormant inside of you for too long. This is our time together."

So, if you are constantly feeling like everyone is getting their happily-ever-after and you are still waiting, you are in great company. This is the season that God wants you all to Himself, so get ready to embrace anonymity. Being hidden requires acceptance. You have to accept that you are not in control of your life. Don't get me wrong—you are a contributor, and God will need your obedience to get you to the destination, but you are not in control. This is God's opportunity to get you into position, and in order to do that, He has to have your undivided attention.

So be prepared to be uncomfortable. Be prepared for God to not tell you a single thing about what He is going to do next. Where you were normally the person someone had on speed dial, be prepared for some silence. Where you were the first person that people would call to hang out, be prepared to go it alone. Where you normally had to bat all of the advances with a stick, be prepared to feel unnoticed and unimportant. Be prepared to be invisible. Seen by God, but hidden from the world. Sometimes that is just the way He likes it.

Please understand that just because you are in a season of quiet does not mean that God has forgotten you. On the contrary, this is the best example of God remembering you. God choosing to hide your greatness from the world is His way of refining you for the greatest season of your life. The confusing thing about God is that what He is doing never actually looks like the outcome. Shake your desire for things to appear a certain way. You will be looking at the way things look and panicking without knowing that God is using difficult and lonely seasons to pull out His absolute best in you.

Let me explain. Years ago, I had to walk through a humiliating season, and I seemed to have lost everything—my church, my friends, and even my marriage. It could not have gotten any uglier. I was at the bottom of the barrel. I seemed to be a master at making situations that were bad—really bad. I had experienced so much hypocrisy in my life that I wanted nothing to do with God or His people.

On the heels of a pretty ugly breakup, I found myself in a really uncomfortable place. My head was swirling, and my heart was destroyed. You see, I was a failure—and not just once but twice! I could not believe that this was my life; things that happened to me weren't supposed to happen. I thought I did everything right. I would canvas my life over and over again. It began pretty simply, I would think. I mean, if I really thought about it all, I have had hard times but nothing that I thought would lead me here...

And here I was... in the gutter. As I reflect on my relationships, I knew I had a problem. In my first attempt at marriage—and I use that term loosely—I thought love had found me. I had waited for marriage until I was 27 years old. He was a strapping military man, and I just knew he was a miracle from God. He waited for me for two years before we got married, and I, in my naiveté, thought that automatically made him a man of God. I was so green to relationships, it never occurred to me that there would ever be the possibility of him being unfaithful.

I still remember where I was when it came out. I was with my maid of honor, and we were doing final arrangements for my wedding. I couldn't leave him now, right? I was devastated! The invitations were mailed, and everyone had attended my shower. My mother was well known; everyone would know, and I could not be an embarrassment to her. Of course he promised never to do it again, so I swallowed my expectations and got married.

Then, at just six months of marriage, February 2004 happened. I remember it like it was yesterday. It was my birthday, and I was scheduled to go to dinner later that night when I received an email at work. It was a very cryptic email, a young lady asking me if I was my husband's sister. She seemed very eager to share with me that she was indeed sleeping with my new husband. How can this be? I read *Your Knight in Shining Armor* by P.B. Wilson! I signed a covenant! This was supposed to turn out right! But it didn't—and I was furious!

I kicked him out of my house. Until I could figure out what to do, I told myself that I would tell my mother, who was in my care at the time, that he was deployed. A short two days later, before I could catch my breath, my mother died. I wanted to die. The only thing keeping me alive was the knowledge that she would want me to live, but at that moment, I did not care about my life anymore.

As if that wasn't sobering enough, just a few short weeks after burying my mother, I found out that I was expecting. I wasn't happy at first. I knew how hard single parenthood was on my mom, and I didn't want that for myself. At the same time, I had been taking care of someone my entire life. I needed someone to take care of, so I was all in with taking care of this beautiful baby. It gave me an escape. I could focus on her instead of all of the hurt in my life, right? Wrong!

At three months pregnant, I was rushed to the hospital for an emergency cerclage. They needed to sew my cervix closed or my daughter would die! Did you hear that? I couldn't fathom that God would allow me to lose my mother and my child in the same year!

That day, I vowed to do whatever I needed to do in order to keep her alive. After many attempts to save her, the doctor admitted me to strict bedrest as an admitted patient in the local hospital. I was there for close to five months, lying in bed, grieving my mother, and trying to keep a baby alive. I was alone, living in a hospital and so numb to life. My child was given only a 2 percent chance at life, and I am grateful to say that she survived.

As a new mom, I recognized our need for more space, so we decided to move. That is when the next level of terror began. In 2005, in the course of packing, I found some bundled envelopes among my mother's things. Inside one of them was a divorce decree for my then-husband to another woman but dated six months after we were married. Imagine the feeling. A flood of emotions covered me. I was done! I was humiliated, and I felt stupid. You mean after all of this, I was not even legally married? I had saved myself for marriage so that I would not have a child out of wedlock, yet here I was! I had to look into the eyes of this beautiful baby that was birthed in a lie. My mother was dead, my wedding… beautiful but my marriage…annulled.

I was destroyed. I know that was the day that I gave up. No, I did not attempt to end my life, but on that day, I allowed hurt to determine every decision I would make going forward. As innocent as it may seem, I placed my life on autopilot. Allowing hurt to drive you will pull you somewhere you do not want to go. I was on a collision course, and I wanted to get as far away from God as I could. Funny how we think we can somehow punish God by walking away from Him. I knowingly entered rebellion, which led me into another relationship that was not pleasing to Him and was ultimately where I hit rock bottom. That is what the enemy does, he will see you at your absolute lowest and go in for the kill!

Later in the book, we will explore this relationship in more detail, but I wanted to show you why I was so barren and why you can take comfort in knowing that God will not leave you that way. In that season, I was so lost that if God spoke to me, I don't know that I would have heard Him. I didn't know His voice anymore, but I was aware that He was the only one who could rescue me.

At the time, YouTube had burst on the scene, and I had become an avid viewer. Not really being taught all of the complexities of the Bible, I was surprised at how much I did not know about the Word of God. I became fascinated with videos that discussed the study of fasting and prayer. Growing up, fasting was something my mother and I did often, so as a long-time faster, I was used to pushing my plate. However, in these studies, I heard it was a surefire way to hear from God, so although the concept of fasting and prayer wasn't new to me, I wasn't very educated on how to do it correctly.

After going through a pretty horrific night of weeping, I truly felt God pulling me to spend forty days before Him in fasting and prayer. I knew spending this amount of time in fasting with the Lord was drastic and I had never attempted something like this before, but I needed to hear His voice. So, I shut everyone out and set out on a journey to find God. I had no choice—I was desperate to hear from Him.

In that time, my whole life began to change. God hurried to my pleas for help, and in just forty days, God spoke to me about ME. So often we ask God to speak to us about a specific issue on our hearts, and instead He decides to reveal to us what we have done to aggravate the situation. In the process, I found myself having to face some pretty radical truths:

1) I did not know God the way I thought I did. In all of my years of serving as a Christian, I really was only acquainted with God. I did not have the true revelation of who He was or what He wanted for me, so I always allowed myself to accept far less than I deserved.

2) I was addicted to the approval of other people. I needed people to affirm whatever I was doing in order to feel validated, successful, and accomplished. This is a bad position to be in because people can be unreliable. If you live your life for their stamp of approval, you will be in constant disarray. Remember, even Jesus had the approval of people, but it didn't take them very long to yell, "Crucify Him!"

3) I put my fate in human hands. I was waiting for someone who was mortal and had no power in my life to change my life for the better. I would become resentful when they would let me down, when what I should have done was taken responsibility for my own happiness looking only to God for help.

4) I had incorrect motives. I used to go above and beyond for people under the pretense of being helpful. When they would take advantage of me I would turn victim and become very hurt. However, when I asked God why this continued to happen to me, he revealed that I really did things for other people because I had a severe need to be needed. I had taken care of other people my entire life and yes, I would give someone the shirt off of my back, but when they did not do the same for me, I would be angry, hurt, and rejected.

God needed to fix all of this in me before He could even begin to address the issues I was going through in my relationships. Of course the skeptic would say, "But if He is God, then He can bless you immediately without your assistance." You are right. However, we need to let go of the expectation that God will ignore what is wrong with us and just give us an instant miracle without requiring that we do the work. Some breakthroughs in our lives require participation in the process. Just because God can do something in spite of us does not mean He should always have to. This helps us to appreciate how far God has brought us. Because we can remember every obstacle we had to overcome in order to get to healing, the knowledge of where we have come from deters us from ever returning back to a broken state.

Hear me out. Sometimes the best healing for our circumstance is a healing that only begins in our souls. For me, this was absolutely the case. I was as needy as they come. I could not even find myself anymore. I had become so entrenched in a relationship because of my unresolved issues that I needed God to unravel the mess I had created. But if we yield to God and allow Him to help us to address all of our emotional issues, some of the issues that we have faced in the past, we will not have to face in the future.

So, what does God do in a time like this? God calls you to a place of solitude. He calls you to embrace Him and hear His voice. I have to admit that when I began this journey with God, I had no idea that the forty days I spent getting to know Him again would only be the beginning of a beautiful new relationship. In the time I invested in God, He took His time with me. He spoke to me. I became a student of the Word and was filled with the Holy Spirit for the first time. He showed me everything I would be giving up if I settled for a life of mediocrity. He promised to awaken every calling that He placed in me before the foundation of the world, and He reminded me that while I had gotten myself in some pretty bad situations, He would turn them around for my good. You see, with God, all the struggles we endure and survive are for purpose. I am not saying that you have to fast for forty days, but if you need to hear God for sure, fasting is how to do it. You can start small—just take a small amount of time each day and dedicate it to God. It will not only change the way you see Him, but it will change your life for the better.

Let's Pray

God, bless my sister—she needs to hear Your voice. Expose her to Your desire for her. Help her to understand You and Your plans for her. Help her to recognize any motive that she may have that is not of You. Help her to know that You are all she needs, and she does not have to put on airs or pretend anymore. Your Word says You desire a broken spirit and a contrite heart. God, break us in the loving way that only You can, so we can be all You have for us to be. Help us to do the work. Show us truth and let us embrace and love it. If we need time in silence with You, then help us to dedicate a time of fasting to You, Lord.

Father, as we push our plates away, incline our ears to hear Your Holy Spirit like we never have before, so that healing can begin. I ask all of these things because of Your love for us. In Jesus's name. Amen!

CHAPTER

2

YOUR HEART

―――――∿∿――――――

> *Above all else, guard your heart, for everything you do flows from it.*
>
> **Proverbs 4:23 NIV**

At some point in our lives, we have all been hurt. We have been betrayed, forgotten, lied to, and misused. Some, not all of us, have some serious heart damage, and we can't begin to receive the love we deserve until we deal with it.

Did you know that your eyes and heart are connected? According to the *European Heart Journal*, "The vasculature of the eye and the heart share several common characteristics. The easily accessible vessels of the eye are therefore—to some extent—a window to the heart" (Flammer et al. 2013). Please do not think I am being overly analytical, but you must see the correlation here. It is a proven scientific fact that your heart and your vision are connected. That being said, when you have heart problems, it is entirely possible for you to end up with vision problems. Knowing that, doesn't that crystalize what most of us have been going through? Some of you are on emotional life support. For you, life has been a battle! You have survived horrific experiences, and because of the damage you have sustained, you have been left with your hearts in ruins, thus leaving your vision impaired.

It is a problem that is more serious than you may realize. If your vision is impaired, you can't see God clearly, so how is it possible for you to have a clear picture of yourself? If we can't see ourselves through His eyes, we can't begin to have an accurate picture of others or his heart for them. Consider this, if I were to ask most of you about an issue in politics or about your personal preferences, you could probably tell me everything you felt about those topics in great detail. With no issues at all, you could recognize the problems and analytically describe what you feel is the solution. But rarely can people see their own issues with such accuracy.

Why is this? Why is it so easy to see things that affect everyone else through a clearer lens than the one that we apply to ourselves? Our vision is the most beautiful yet complex gift that God has given us. Yet, it is the one thing we can't seem to trust. Why are we are so used to second-guessing ourselves that we doubt the very identity that God has given us? You don't need a prophecy for everything! Why does it always take someone else to call things to our attention before we can acknowledge its validity? Whether it's in ministry or otherwise, if you get nothing else from this book, take this with you, you have to have a vision for your own life. Stop waiting for others to tell you what God has already spoken to you. You have to believe Him.

It is my opinion that we have become spoiled in some respects. We are so dependent on the man or woman of God to speak into our lives that we can't make a move without them. I am not saying there isn't a time and place for this type of ministry, but what I am saying is that some of us are using the prophetic as a crutch. Don't you see that doubting yourself is diminishing what God has planted in you? Your purpose in God is not served well by downplaying your gifts, talents, or abilities. Sometimes we can be master encouragers for others but criticize ourselves so much that we can't make a move.

We live in a highly critical society and it has made us approval addicted. People spend hours on end on social media, watching what they assume to be accurate pictures of other people's lives. Our world is changing. There used to be discretion but social media has introduced the world to each other with a few clicks of a button. Suddenly, everyone who wants to speak into your life positively or negatively now has a microphone—and these people are not always nice... Don't believe me? Just spend a day on any social media outlet, and you will have a clear picture of just how critical people can be of someone else's life or circumstances. I am sure you have you seen them. They are the people that are comfortable discussing and dissecting everyone else's situation but can never seem to identify or address items in their own lives that may be falling short.

This is a dangerous place to be in because if you do not have vision for your own life, you will get caught up in all of the chaos. You will be so obsessed with the likes, the shares, and the haters that are trolling you that you will be focused on the incorrect thing. Understand that this frustration and distraction is by design. The enemy knows your purpose, and he wants it at all costs. If he can surround you 24/7 with negativity then you will be so inundated with defending yourself or getting on your personal soapbox that you will not have time to fulfill the work. You have to open your eyes. You can't afford to remain in the dark about who you are in Christ. The enemy wants you as discouraged and self-critical as possible. If he can use outlets like this to get you to that place, then it is much easier for him to make you project that behavior onto others. Either way, it is a win-win for him.

I submit to you that if you can't see yourself as clearly as you think you can see others, whether it is positive or negative, then you may have a heart problem. You could be forming opinions and seeing certain situations through the lens of your hurt. Take special care to examine a matter. Before you post that comment, write that email, or even make that phone call, you need to ask yourself, "Why do I see it this way?"

For instance, my beautiful daughter is involved in school sports. Every so often, in order to participate, she has to get a physical. One year, I took her to the doctor as per usual, and things seemed to be going well. Until the vision test. That is when this story takes a turn for the worst. She was reading the letters on the eye chart and appeared to be doing it with ease. But then the doctor said to her, "Now, let's test the other eye." All of a sudden, she became flustered, frustrated, and surprised—she could not see anything! In order to pass the examination, she needed 20/20 vision, and my then twelve-year-old daughter, who thought her vision was fine, was devastated to learn that she had 20/50 vision—and that wasn't good enough to play basketball without glasses. When she realized that she had failed the examination, she immediately began to panic, making excuses and asking the doctor and me to take her side.

"But, Mom, I can see fine in the other eye! Why is having both eyes exactly the same so important anyway?" she cried.

She was so discouraged, and as a mother, it was difficult to watch. Then her doctor had to explain the importance of visual balance. She explained that by not being able to see on the court, she wasn't only endangering herself, but everyone around her.

I use this example to drive home to you that as women of God, we have to have visual balance. Ask yourself the following questions: *Can I see clearly? What is the state of my heart? Is it in working order? Have I dealt with everything that has happened to me? Are there any unresolved issues that I have not addressed with God? Is there bitterness that may be sitting down on the inside of me?* If you have not asked yourself these questions at some point in your walk with God, chances are that you have not taken the time to address your heart issues. And if you have not addressed them, it is entirely possible that you can't see clearly the man that God has for you, either. In the same way you deserve to be hidden from men who may hurt you, your man of God deserves to be hidden from you until God is sure that you will not hurt him.

I understand that these are hard questions and, depending on the answers, there may be some healing that needs to take place, but it is unrealistic for you to require a man to heal you. That is a transaction that should take place between you and God. For years, we have created in our minds these faux fairy tales of who our Prince Charming would be, how much money he would make, and where our kingdom would be located. But this is no Disney movie. No man is scaling a wall and fighting a dragon to rescue you from your own mess, so do away with that form of thinking because it is unfair. Scale your own wall or, better yet, ask the Holy Spirit to break every stronghold you have erected in your life, so your relationships begin on equal footing.

Furthermore, I don't expect that you should rescue him, either. You both have one Savior. Take responsibility and ask God to heal you and to soften your heart. When your heart is in order, then you will see clearly, and God can reveal you to the one you are waiting for. Your relationship of purpose deserves a fighting chance.

How Do We Heal?

Healing your heart is one of the most tedious stages of the process. While you are in your hidden season, you are going to find that God will reveal some things in your character that are not pleasing to Him. He is going to use this up-close and personal time to expose some of the walls the enemy has erected in your life. As He speaks to you, get ready for Him to move some things around. He never had any intention of allowing you to stay the same. He is your Father, and He loves you enough to show you where you need improvement, so change is necessary. It is God's desire that we become the best representation of Him; we will never be perfect, but we can strive toward perfection.

Philippians 3:13–14 (KJV) says: "Brethren, I count not myself to have apprehended: but this one thing I do, forgetting those things which are behind, and reaching forth unto those things which are before, I press toward the mark for the prize of the high calling of God in Christ Jesus." It does not matter if you are single or married, a career woman or a volunteer in your community. If you are claiming to be a woman of God, then your mandate is one of service, and HE will make you fit for His use. He will change you, soften you, and make you ready for the next season.

Singleness is the perfect time to be molded by your Father into what He needs you to be. Your communication with Him is imperative and essential to the healing process. Knowing what God desires of you will require that you are sensitive to the Holy Spirit and able to hear His voice. So if you have not cultivated this aspect of your relationship with God, then you, my dear, are ill equipped to hear Him clearly or recognize your sent man. May I suggest that you work on your relationship with God first before you seek to be sought out by your man of purpose? You must remember that God not only loves you, but He loves your future spouse as well. It is his job to protect you both and if you are not ready, he will not send him. But for argument's sake, let's say that you feel that you are ready. You are serving, running hard after God and wanting His best for your life. That's good. Let's explore some areas where the enemy tends to hide our deficiencies and see if we are really ready. Let's go!

Forgiveness. I feel like about 100 of you cringed when you read that word. Personally, it is an area of our lives that we would just as soon ignore. You would think that after all the years of teaching that the church has done on the subject, we would be better in this area, but we aren't. We just can't seem to progress, and I wonder why that is.

The short answer is because it is hard! I am not proud to say that this has been a heart lesson that God has had to baby-step me through, as I am no stranger to hurt. I wish I could say that the majority of the pain that I have endured were from random atheists, but unfortunately most of the hurt I suffered was in the church. I have experienced more slander, backbiting, and betrayal from so-called believers than I care to acknowledge, and some of it was absolutely gut-wrenching. I mean, these are the people who are supposed to know better, and to experience intentional acts of cruelty because of jealousy, insecurity, and a host of other issues? I was done!

I can remember on more than one occasion telling God that as much as I loved Him, I was done with His people and it took a lot to teach me forgiveness. I had no idea that in my case, God would use situations that put me in a position to forgive over and over to teach me how to triumph in those circumstances. You see, I was no forgiveness pro. If someone misused me, then I wanted them to pay—I felt like forgiving them was letting them off the hook. However, it was really releasing me.

Nine times out of ten, the root of unforgiveness is pride. Forgiveness is just releasing our need to right a wrong or feel vindicated and walking away from something that tried to take us out and failed. Notice I said it failed? We can't allow the enemy the satisfaction of keeping us shackled to that dead situation. Unforgiveness keeps you in the pit, and we are getting out of there today! First Peter 2:9 (NIV) says: "But you are a chosen people, a royal priesthood, a holy nation, God's special possession, that you may declare the praises of him who called you out of darkness into his wonderful light." Girl, you are royalty! We have too much to do in the kingdom to be pulled off of our thrones by an act of peasantry like unforgiveness. God has people for that. We don't even tolerate it in our position; we can't afford to.

So how do we do it? How do we push past all of the wrongdoing? First, I had to get over myself and forgive. It has been a long, tedious process—and God has had to correct me more than once—but through it came revelation and I would love to share it with you.

Mark 11:25 (NIV) says: "And when you stand praying, if you hold anything against anyone, forgive them, so that your Father in heaven may forgive you your sins." You know that there have been times when you have done things that God was not pleased with, and I am sure we have all needed forgiveness at one time or another. Remember, God has no fellowship with darkness. We can't walk in the light with deception in our hearts, and if you are walking in unforgiveness, you are deceived. Failing to forgive others hinders God's ability to forgive you. We have to remember that God literally has to forgive us every single day.

Sometimes I feel that people in the church (in general) come to God and change their lives, and then act like they don't remember what they used to do before God saved them. Don't get saved and then get amnesia. Trust me, I am in no way suggesting that you are to participate in activities around you that pull you out of your deliverance, but I am saying that you should lighten up. You remember some of the things that you have done, and God was faithful enough to cover it up so that no one found out. That was only because of His grace, and we have to remember that when we decide to condemn others who have done us wrong. God is faithful, and He will address all of the matters of your heart, but you have to be honest with him. Come clean, then ask Him to help you forgive. God does not expect you to be able to do it without His assistance. Again, ask Him to help you forgive so He can forgive you and you can move on.

Shhhh…

Do not let any unwholesome talk come out of your mouths, but only what is helpful for building others up according to their needs, that it may benefit those who listen. And do not grieve the Holy Spirit of God, with whom you were sealed for the day of redemption. Get rid of all bitterness, rage and anger, brawling and slander, along with every form of malice. Be kind and compassionate to one another, forgiving each other, just as in Christ God forgave you.

(Ephesians 4:29–32, NIV)

In other words, hush! Stop talking about it. If you can't speak life to the situation, do not speak! I used to be a major offender of this one. When I went through some of the most difficult seasons of my life, I thought that people needed an understanding of the wrongdoing. I believed that if they knew the truth, they would automatically understand my actions and act accordingly, but I will tell you something that is going to blow your mind. A lot of the time, people do not care about the truth, and you can't take that personally. People are fickle. It's not that they don't care about you, they just don't care about anything that doesn't directly benefit them.

Pour out Your Heart to God

I understand that it can be so easy to pour out our hearts to people because they are right in front of us. We don't see God every day, so we use people as our outlet, and we bleed to them instead of taking our issues to God. But you must remember that people are human and are only capable of so much. Expecting to not be hurt by people is unfair. It is not a question of what you will do *if* people disappoint you, but a question of what you will do *when* people disappoint you.

By default, you should be taking the matters of your heart to God first! He is big enough to handle everything possible thing you could throw at him. With the exception of psychologists who have been trained to be supportive and discreet, most human beings are not always in a place in their lives where they can handle your secrets. In addition, they do not all deserve to be placed in a position to know everything about you. A big problem we tend to have is that we share information with people who have shown us who they are, and then we are shocked when they do what their character has already displayed in previous situations. Don't lose hope! You can protect yourself, but it begins by identifying who God has placed in your life to be your safe haven. If you know you can trust them, feel free to use them as an outlet, but if there is any part of you that is unsure, leave those matters for God and Him alone.

Later in the book, we will talk about wise counsel, but for now, let's get back to the thing hindering your forgiveness: your mouth! Ask yourself these questions: *Have I truly forgiven? If I have, why would I want to breathe life back into a dead situation by putting my voice on it?* Let me explain. No matter how bad things may seem or how hopeless the position you are in, God will vindicate you. He has given you the most powerful tool you will ever use in this life to defeat your foe.

In Proverbs 18:21 (KJV), the Word of God says, "Death and life are in the power of the tongue: and they that love it shall eat the fruit thereof." Your tongue is powerful. You have been given the power to breathe life into the situations you are facing and destroy the enemy's plot against you, but either way, remember this: whatever you speak, it will be you that eats the fruit of it. You have to let it go, and that means not discussing it anymore. God is not a God who falls asleep on the job. He knows what they said about you. He knows they lied, and He knows the hurt inflicted upon you was unfair. Take comfort in knowing that God has a wonderful memory, and He will not sit by and allow you to be mistreated. God revealed a couple of things to me about my mouth in similar situations. Allow me to share them with you, as I know it has helped me tremendously.

You cannot truly forgive someone and defame them at the same time. If you are pleading with the Lord to help you forgive someone, it is better not to speak about them at all than to allow yourself to be drawn into a conversation with someone who will invite you to rehash the situation over and over again. This is not accidental. Think about it. Of all the people that the other person could have called about why they were frustrated, they called you. Could it be because they were hurt and wanted someone to get in their pit of misery with them for a little mudslinging?

Sweetheart, when God cleans you up, you don't jump back into a hogpen for anybody. If they choose to roll around in the pit in their best Sunday attire, you better not join them—and when people bring that mess to you, do not be silent! Make a declaration that you are over that situation and you don't even want to talk about it anymore. I promise they will never mention it to you again. It is important to remind yourself that speaking about a dead situation is just another way for you to rally troops to fight a war that only God can fight! God had to remind me that He loves His children, all of them, even the ones who hurt me, and when I was speaking against them, I was actually speaking against Him. He is just as jealous for them as He is for me. God will not sit by and allow you to speak against His children and then turn around and vindicate you! When you are rehashing all of your old hurts, is that God speaking? Or is that the enemy's means of keeping you in the same place?

My suggestion to you is to stay in the safe zone. You do not need to take revenge on your enemies, that is dangerous territory. Just let God exercise his wrath, trust me, it will be enough. Romans 12:19 (NIV) says, "'It is mine to avenge; I will repay,' says the Lord." Unforgiveness pulls us down to the same level as the one who has subjected us to the wrongdoing. When we participate in petty retaliation, then we sign up to reap some of those consequences ourselves.

Unforgiveness at its very root is just plain ole pride dressed up in a different outfit! Let's be honest, you don't want to forgive because you don't want them to get away with what they did to you. Love, I assure you, God never intends to allow them to just get away with their actions. As a parent, I can say that I have learned one thing, if nothing else: I extend grace to my daughter when she does wrong, but I do not always allow her to escape the consequences. Nine times out of ten, the lesson comes by working through the consequence.

As a parent, no one has more authority over my child than I do, and no other child can come into my house and overrule me. God is no different. He has all authority whether we accept it or not. He will not allow one child to overrule Him in the discipline of another.

Forgiveness at its core is a radical act of trust in God. You either believe God or you don't. When you refuse to forgive, you tell God that you do not believe He is willing or able to vindicate you. Think about that. If you really believed that God was doing His job, then you would have no problem letting go.

You can't allow your fear to rule you. You letting God have a situation and then picking it back up again is not trust, it is fear! Real trust is giving God the situation and telling Him that you trust Him to make it right, even if it does not look like He will fix it the way you want Him to. Don't allow yourself to be so consumed with making the other party pay that you are willing to sacrifice who you are in God. When we don't see God moving on our timetable, we can get antsy and start trying to intervene in His business, but the moment you ask Him to help you forgive, that situation is no longer your business. So, give it to him and move on.

How Are People Supposed to Love Me?

I often hear women say things like: "I can't believe he did this to me. Didn't he love me?" I have a hard time with these questions because I think this way of thinking is a snare. Whether or not someone loves you is the wrong question. The question is not *if* they love you, but if they are capable of loving you at the level you truly deserve. In spite of all of their negative experiences, have they asked God to restore them to the point that they are capable of offering love in a way that resonates with you? What is their capacity to love another human being?

When I considered the idea of people being able to offer love at equal levels, this became super personal for me, because it would be one of the last lessons my mother would ever teach me before she went home to be with the Lord. You see, I am the product of a single-parent home. My parents split when I was just 11 months old, so I did not know what family looked like. My mother was a talented singer, and she made ends meet as well as she could. She was always very encouraging to me and was the center of all I had. I knew for sure who my biological father was, as he made cameo appearances every once in a while. But for the most part, he was absent.

My mother was a domestic violence survivor who had seen a really ugly side of love. She lost teeth, suffered broken ribs, and had scars from knife wounds. But every day she wore them as a badge of honor and a testament to the goodness of God. She had been through the wringer, and as a result, she demanded respect. Knowing the sacrifices that she made for me, I gladly gave it to her, but what I could not understand was her reinforcing the need for me to respect my father. I mean, he wasn't even there. How could I respect someone who was absent? That is like someone telling you to make dinner for an invisible man. Growing up, I would get so angry with her, and for a while it did take its toll on our relationship. I just could not understand why she demanded that I love my father. He was no angel, and if anyone had reason to hate him, it was her. And yet at every given opportunity, she would defend my father. All I had to go on was a life of disappointment, missed play dates, and broken promises.

One of my most painful memories was when I was getting married. My father called and said he wanted to be involved. He gave this big speech and said that he wanted to make things right because he was never there for me. Of course, in true fashion, my mother believed him. It took a while, but he eventually won me over. Then it happened. A whopping two days before my wedding, when he was supposed to provide his portion of the wedding expenses and give me away, he was a no-show. Not just a no-show financially, but a physical no-show! Here I was, looking at my soon-to-be husband who had his entire family come in from another state, and my father stood me up the day of my rehearsal dinner!

I was embarrassed, humiliated, and even angry—with my mom! You see, I had settled into life without him. God had sent me a surrogate. At birth, my godfather stepped into my life and had been everything I needed, so I had no expectations of my biological father at all. Then all of a sudden this happens, and I was drowning in memories of that seven-year-old little girl who sat on the couch for three days in her favorite outfit, waiting for her father to show up. I was livid, and based on my behavior, I would venture to say I temporarily lost my mind. In a fit of rage, I yelled at my mother; I think this was the only day in my life that I was bold enough to do that!

"Why do you make me respect him?" I yelled. "Why did you teach me to love him? Don't you understand how painful it was for him not to be able to reciprocate?"

My mother just shook her head and sat quietly. Personally, I was shocked that she did not club me with her cane. Then with a half scowl and side-eye smile, she said, "Stupid, stupid girl. You think I taught you to love him, for him? So he would benefit? I taught you to love him for you! My job is to teach you to love furiously, even if that love can't be returned. Lisa, your father had problems growing up. He loved me to the best level HE could love me, and he loves you—even in his absence—to the best level he can love you." It wasn't until her death, a short six months later, that I truly understood that statement.

We are taught to love. If we are taught to love big, we love big! If we are taught to love selfishly, we love selfishly. If we are taught to be giving, we are giving. And if we are taught to be takers, then guess what? We are takers. Unfortunately, what a lot of parents do not realize is that their actions teach their kids far more than their words.

Loving someone is a risk. When you are vulnerable, you are giving someone permission to hurt you completely if they aren't capable of loving you at your level. It is all about their capacity to love. You can expect love all day, but people can only love you at the capacity that they are capable of loving, and you have to decide if that level works for you. I have been in situations where I was downright angry that I gave more in a relationship than I received. Now I realize that I got everything back that the person could or would give anyone. It just wasn't love at my level.

You can't change or modify how someone loves you. You can set an expectation, but ultimately, that person is going to determine how they are going to love you. You have to be realistic; if you are currently in a relationship and feel unloved, then you have some decisions to make, because that person may be genuinely giving you everything they are capable of giving anyone. A lot of us believe that the way we are loved has everything to do with us, but usually this is not the case. If the person we love so much is unable to reciprocate, it can seem like we are the problem; we may even feel like we are unlovable.

Ladies, we are so hard on ourselves, we begin the negative self-talk and play messages in our heads over and over again. Sometimes we even think the reason that we are not in loving relationships is because we are expecting too much, but that is not true. Could it be that you may be with someone who is so hurt that they are incapable of showing love? On some level, I believe my mother was correct. Someone may not be loving you the way you need them to, but you must accept that they are loving you from where they are. Unfortunately, in some cases, that may mean not at all. Some people just do not know how to love and people can't genuinely love others unless they first truly love themselves.

Love is a taught behavior. There is something so elementary to it. However, if you and your partner have had love displayed for you in different ways, you will both have a different understanding of what love looks like. If you are someone who believes that someone who truly loves you shows that love by constant affection, but the other person was raised in a home where affection was neither expressed nor encouraged, you will become frustrated. If you are currently in a relationship and do not feel loved, I believe that you should examine your relationship again. Take out the personal feelings you may have associated with them and look at them for what they are.

Don't shoot the messenger. I am not saying that you should detach from them, but I am asking you to take a hard look at your relationship without allowing your personal feelings to be involved and ask yourself, *Is this person loving me at a level I can deal with forever?* If you are not comfortable with that answer, then you have some changes to make. Do not marry someone thinking that you are going to change how they express love.

Side note: If you are in an unsafe relationship, then you must leave immediately! You can't change someone with anger, mental, or spiritual abuse issues. God has to fix that person, and that person can't want to be fixed for you. They have to want it for themselves. But if you are in a relationship with someone who can't express love and you need more from them, then have the faith to believe your God for more, even if it is not with that person. (This advice is fully transferable and can apply to all relationships.)

I know that we are in an era where blocking people is the norm; immediately some of you have this visual of kicking everyone you are unhappy with out of your life, but that is not entirely what I mean. Don't get me wrong—if the shoe fits, strap on that shoe and run a mile in it! But for others, I am saying you need to let some people off the hook. Some of you have internalized the emotions associated with these relationships so much that you are believing that their lack of ability to love you is about you, when it is actually about them and their deficiencies.

Let's analyze my relationship with my dad a little closer. It wasn't until I attempted to truly examine my relationship with my father that I understood why my expectations of him were unreasonable, I was probably the only woman in history who was intentionally raised to be a daddy's girl to an absent father. However, his absence never stopped me from loving him or even wanting him to be proud of me.

But there was a problem; clearly, my vision was impaired. You see, based on my perception, I always saw him as this successful man who rejected me. I saw a man who willingly raised two other children but left me by the road like yesterday's garbage. What I didn't see was a man who was at his capacity. He loved me. But he loved me the way HE could love me. I don't know all of the details about his difficult upbringing, but I do know that it not only shaped him but defined the kind of father he would be—and ultimately the level of love he could give to anyone. This revelation changed everything. Suddenly he wasn't this absentee dad anymore; I saw a bruised, broken, and bitter man dealing with the blows that life had given him.

Without warning, I was overtaken by a flood of emotions. I didn't know where to begin. You see, around my sixteenth birthday, I decided to turn all of those feelings off. I just didn't want to hurt anymore, so I decided that I would bury all of my feelings of rejection and disillusionment. I told myself that maybe if I just forgot him, all of the pain would go away. For those of you who have suffered from a severed relationship on any level, you know that the hurt can be unbearable. So, I vowed never to feel anything for him again.

But this new feeling was indescribable and a little weird. It was scary, fun, and foreign. I felt! For the first time in a great while, I suddenly knew what it was like to feel again. I felt a love for my father that I had locked away for more than twenty years because I had allowed rejection to build a shell around the love I was taught to give. Real love, the kind our Father gives, changes us. Drowning in these new emotions, I quickly became

47

aware of a glaring fact: I was taught by a loving mother to love deeply, and he was not. He didn't know any better, but I did.

Once I digested this new information and processed these new feelings, I had an epiphany! His absence wasn't about me at all! It was about him and his ability, or his lack thereof, to love. He was only loving me the way he could, and that needed to be enough—even if it wasn't adequate for me. I had to accept that he was at capacity, and just like that, I let him off the hook! I officially allowed myself to free him of any responsibility for my happiness and decided to move on. I had to take responsibility for my happiness and realize that I was only orphaned if I decided to declare and accept that identity for myself.

We must be careful. We need to acknowledge the hurt but not identify with it. You are not hurt! You *were* hurt! You are not broken! You *were* broken. There is a huge difference. So, when I decided to face the fact that although he decided to walk away, it was me who would decide what would occur in my future, I was able to accept his absence and his capacity to love me.

Love is acceptance. Sometimes it is accepting that the person you desire to feel love from just can't love you the way you need it. Many of us could live peaceful and fulfilled lives if we could accept that some rejection in our lives has nothing to do with us. You refusing to accept someone's love capacity not only does you a disservice, but it also keeps the other person in a constant state of frustration and failure because they feel like they will never meet your expectations. If they are not right for you, then you have to move on and allow them to find someone that can accept them as they are. Sweetheart, you owe it to yourself to open yourself up for the right relationship. Some people just aren't going to be able to meet your expectations, and that is okay because there is someone out there who will.

Second Corinthians 6:14 (KJV) says, "Be ye not unequally yoked together with unbelievers: for what fellowship hath righteousness with unrighteousness? and what communion hath light with darkness?" This scripture is so misunderstood. This truth is not meant to limit you, it is meant to liberate you. It is meant to keep you safe. God knew that you being with someone who does not match your purpose would cause you hurt and frustration. If you are a physically expressive person, you can't be in a close relationship with someone who isn't; you will be frustrated every time. So stop settling, and stop allowing society or invisible timetables make you take whatever is available.

If you are in a relationship and you just can't accept the level of love being shown to you, get out! You deserve the very best, and God has that for you. I am speaking to singles only. Please don't take this as a license to jump out of marriage—this is a singles book. If you know that the person you love is doing what they can, and they genuinely see change needs to occur and are willing to make the necessary changes, then you have something to work with. I repeat, the other person has a desire to change *without* you requiring it. That means no ultimatums, no pronouncements, and no theatrics. Allow them to hear your thoughts and let them take the necessary steps. If they are willing to do the work on themselves, then you can move forward and let them off the hook. Even if you realize that there is no future for this relationship, remember this: forgive, love, and let go. It doesn't just release them—it releases you!

Dealing with Disappointments

How many times have you been haunted by disappointment? I am sure we can all think back to a time when we thought something was going to happen a certain way at a certain time, only to be disappointed and frustrated that our plans did not work out. In your hidden season, you must remember that our timing and God's timing aren't the same. I know you know that, but I just need to remind someone who is still toiling with a disappointment that they had no control over.

Listen to me, even when you think you are in control, you aren't. God has made you an intelligent being. I do not doubt for one minute the vast giftings and callings He has placed in you, but you must also be careful. Sometimes because we are so gifted, we can go about our plans and not consult Him. But with God, you must always make sure that your plans are first subject to His plans for your life, and trust me, I know it is hard. As a single woman, I can't tell you how many times I have heard a friend say, "I thought I would have a baby by now," or "I thought I would own a house by now," or "I just knew I would be married by now." I know it is hard to wait.

Earlier I mentioned these invisible timetables that we have. I am no different. When I was twenty-one years old, I had my life mapped and a two-page list of everything that should happen and when. I remember being devastated on my twenty-third birthday when I didn't see the fruits of the promises God made me. Ah, to be young again. I would do so much differently, starting with allowing God to direct my life without my intervention, but I digress.

We have to make sure that we are checking in with God to see if what we are doing is what He wants. I wasn't close enough to God at the time to even ask the question, and as a result, I have many dreams that were deferred. Sometimes we allow disappointments to stop our progress. If you are anything like me, I began to believe that it was too late for me to achieve the things that I knew God had told me. But I am so grateful that God is a God of truth, and if He makes you a promise and you are still breathing, it's not too late! Romans 11:29 (NLT) says, "For God's gifts and his call can never be withdrawn." My sister in Christ, take courage in knowing that God plans to do just what He said.

Do not hesitate—get started today! If God has spoken something over your life, you should not be waiting until you are married to be working on it. In some cases, your lackadaisical attitude may be what is delaying the arrival of your sent man! Let's imagine that just maybe God is holding him in one position for you to pass by, but you never get there because the meeting is on the other side of your service to God. Imagine saying, "Well, I was hurt in this relationship, and although I know I am called to serve the elderly, I am too hurt to go on." Then one day in your obedience to God, you walk into an assisted living facility and bump into what will later be your husband! I am not saying that God gives you purpose so that you can bump into your mate, nor am I suggesting that God has these types of limitations, but what I am saying is if you know God is leading you in a direction, then go! You have no idea what He has in store for you, but worrying or meditating on past mistakes is robbing you of today.

Philippians 4:6–7 (NKJV) says: "Be anxious for nothing, but in everything by prayer and supplication, with thanksgiving, let your requests be made known to God; and the peace of God, which surpasses all understanding, will guard your hearts and minds through Christ Jesus." If you want God's peace to rule, then you must surrender every disappointment to Him. You will find that when you truly give it all to Him, you will finally have His peace.

The first thing you have to realize is that you have nothing to prove. You tried something, and it failed. Try again. When asked, Thomas A. Edison said, "I have not failed. I've just found 10,000 ways that won't work." What an outlook! Can you imagine what we could achieve if we just tried things without the fear of failing? Who made us so afraid to make mistakes anyway? Jesus died for your mistakes! If you were in a relationship and humiliated, pray and then love again. If you had a close friend who betrayed you, turn it over and let God repay your enemies. Some of you were in a relationship and thought this one was "the one," and for reasons beyond your control, it has ended. Don't allow your disappointment to take you back into the wilderness you were in. Understand that God has better for you, so keep moving forward.

You hear me? Keep moving! Trust that the Lord your God is your keeper, and He is never asleep on the job. He is awake and burning the midnight oil looking for ways to bless you, His beautiful daughter. Remember that even in your disappointment, God will give you the strength to accomplish in Him what you never dreamed you could on your own. Because He is your Shepherd, you can do all that He has graced you to do. There is no dream you can imagine that is impossible for God. You can and will accomplish anything because God promises to go before you if you let Him. What I love most about God being God is that He is not unaware of what it feels like to be human. He knows what hurt feels like, He knows what pain feels like, and He is there to soothe every emotional, spiritual, and physical ache you may have. Don't allow the enemy to make you turn your focus to your failures. Your disappointments are what make your testimony that much more powerful, so fail on, baby girl! God has a blessing with your name on it!

Real Love Doesn't Hurt

One of the hardest seasons in my life was when I was faced with abuse. Abuse in any form is detestable. We are suffering every day and, in most cases, suffering silently. We have allowed ourselves to accept treatment that is so far beneath what God has planned for us that it is heartbreaking. Abuse is often overlooked in the church, and I can understand why no one would want to talk about it. I don't agree, but I understand. What is even more shocking are those of you who are in abusive relationships right now and don't even realize it.

So, what is abuse? According to the *Merriam-Webster* dictionary, one definition of abuse is "physical maltreatment." However, there are so many types of abuse. There is, of course, physical abuse; this type of abuse can include anything that strikes fear of physical harm to the victim. According to reachma.org, physical abuse usually entails "punching, hitting, slapping, kicking, strangling, or physically restraining a partner against their will. It can also include driving recklessly or invading someone's physical space, and in any other way making someone feel physically unsafe."

Our first problem is using the media as the primary point of reference for abuse. Of course, the movies we have seen makes abuse look only one way. There is this big, strong man who has a checkered past that no one knows about, and then one day he just snaps and beats his wife. That is the way it always is, right? Wrong. Abuse never looks like that in the beginning. It didn't for me. For me, it was veiled and very well hidden. It was a moment when all seemed to be going well, and something seemed to upset him that had nothing to do with me. He would become angry with a person, and when he couldn't express his anger to that party, I was the recipient.

In my case, it would be unfair to insinuate that the abuse was physical right away. Quite the contrary, it started out as a controlling streak. It would be a phone call, and if I (a working woman) wasn't able to reach him back right away, it turned to text messages. One message expressed what may have seemed to others as genuine concern, but if I didn't answer fast enough, that concern quickly escalated to multiple text messages per hour and calling me disrespectful names. When he was finally able to reach me, he wasn't very apologetic; it was more like a reprimand for not being available during the workday.

If you have never been with someone who is controlling, then I can't say that you would know what to look for. You see, this was only the second long-term relationship I had in my life. When I would push back, the flowers would come and he'd say, "I am sorry, I am just going through a lot right now." Of course, as a Christian woman, I needed to be compassionate, right? This was a side to him I had never seen, so that couldn't be who he really was. I was deceived and very naïve. When you are with someone and they suddenly become another person, that should show you that this person has some variation of a personality disorder or at the very minimum is pretending to be someone they are not. Controlling behavior is not the result of a bad day or life circumstances. It is unacceptable, and you should rethink the relationship.

I wish I could say that at that stage of my relationship, I trusted myself enough to care about my well-being, but I didn't. You see, abusers are never evil in the beginning. They are kind and they are sweet; they love everything you love, and you think that you have found your best friend. (Side note: This is why I often tell people to be careful when they refer to their mate as their best friend.)

It is okay to desire—of course we all want that—but there can be another side to that dynamic that is rarely discussed. You see, if I was a calculated and narcissistic person, as abusers often are, then I would study my subject and create similarity, so they have a false sense of security. So of course, he is your best friend; that is what he has to be to get close to you. You will slowly begin to notice that he wants more and more of your time. Your time with your friends will greatly diminish, and perhaps even time with your family will become scarce. Do you know why? Because it is very hard to abuse someone who has a tribe of people concerned about their well-being, this man's goal is to be your everything. He does not want to share you so if he can get you into isolation, then he can deceive you into believing that all you really have is him. Mission accomplished!

Do you see why this is a topic that we don't want to discuss in the kingdom? We can talk about sex, adultery, homosexuality, hatred, and even money, but we do not want to talk about abuse. Why can't we talk about it? In short, the answer is timidity. Some churches are more concerned about the dynamics of their financial well-being, because of course every dollar counts. Some pastors will even go as far as to advise that you stay because the Bible never speaks on abuse, so technically God never says a man should not abuse his wife. In short, we make the decision to keep silent. Meanwhile, the same tithers that they are so concerned about losing are dying at a rapid rate.

According to an article in the *HuffPost*, "the number of American troops killed in Afghanistan and Iraq between 2001 and 2012 was 6,488. The number of American women who were murdered by current or ex male partners during that time was 11,766. That's nearly *double* the number of casualties lost during *war*." Every year in the U.S., 4,774,000 women experience physical violence by an intimate partner. That is astounding, and the churchgoers are just over there taking Communion and singing worship songs. Silence is consent if we, as the church, are not willing to speak out against violence. If we are encouraging our parishioners to stay in relationships with people that will kill them for the sake of preserving our idea of the family, how can we say we represent God? No matter how you try to spin it, if you affirm or conceal the behavior, you are complicit. Remember, Jesus was an activist against injustice so when we, as the church, keep silent on matters such as these, who are we representing?

According to the same article, one in four women will be victims of abuse from a significant other in their lifetime, and one in seven men will experience the same. Can we realistically say that none of these people attend church? Believe me, I would love to tell you that abuse is not taking place in the church because we know and value Jesus and His love for all people, but that would be untrue. We do not prioritize people anymore; we tell women that if they fight back, then they are not really being abused. But, love, I am here to tell you that if a man hits you or abuses you in any way, you have every right to defend yourself. You do not have to sit by while they decide to lay hands on you. If you defend yourself, yes, you are still a victim. Why? Because although a woman can defend herself, she should not have to. The Word of God says, "Husbands, love your wives, just as Christ loved the church and gave himself up for her" (Ephesians 5:25, NIV). Sis, Jesus loved you so much that He died for you. He would never allow you to be hurt. He would never want you to bring yourself so low that you would accept treatment that He Himself would not subject you to.

When I think about how many murders have happened that could have been prevented, I am saddened. No one deserves abuse. No matter how innocent it appears at the onset, if someone is hurting you, please know that all the theology in the world will not save you from it. But God, who loves you and wants an abundant life for you, says that you are more than good enough, and He will not stand by while someone destroys His child.

If you are dating, you may think you are immune to this, but trust me, you are not. Please get to know the person you are in a relationship with, and if a red flag is waving, seek wise counsel, and then take that counsel's advice and lay it at the feet of Jesus. If you solely rely only on the opinions of people, they will have you in danger and it won't affect them at all, because they are not dealing with what you are dealing with. I wish that someone would have told me when I was dating that abuse looks different for everyone. Had I known what to look for during the dating period, a wedding never would have happened.

I truly believe that this issue should be addressed in marital counseling, and of course as I write this, I can already hear some of you saying, "Lisa, he doesn't hit me. He just says really hurtful things." Well, my love, that is emotional abuse, and the emotional abuser is in some ways more dangerous than the physical attacker. This abuser wants to do nothing more than break you! As a single woman, if you are dating a man who likes to take little jabs at you or say little things here and there to hurt you, end it now. Remember that by taking his hand in marriage, you are affirming his behaviors—good and bad—and while you are not consenting to his abuse, he may continue to abuse you because you married him knowing that he was abusive. Marriage does not make things better; it affirms things you already know are present.

An abusive man will chip away at everything you are if you are not careful. His goal is to do everything possible to get into your head and project his own personal insecurities onto you and before you know it, you are doing everything possible to please him. He will not be second, even to God. It is an entertaining game for him; meanwhile, you are in turmoil. I am here to tell you that, no, you are not crazy. You are just as you should be, but half of an abuser's job is to have you so downcast that you can't see what is real and what is fake anymore. On a deeper level, I wish I could tell you that all you need to be is angry at the abuser, but that is not true. He is a mere pawn in this battle. The Word of God says, "For we wrestle not against flesh and blood, but against principalities, against powers, against the rulers of the darkness of this world, against spiritual wickedness in high places. Wherefore take unto you the whole armor of God, that ye may be able to withstand in the evil day, and having done all, to stand" (Ephesians 6:12–13, KJV).

Please understand that a man's predisposition to abuse has nothing to do with you. He is not pretending to be an abuser, and he is not just having abusive moments; the man he is when he pretends to be nice to you is the imposter. That is the man who is not genuine, the persona he has created to get you in his clutches. The abusive man is who he really is.

I am telling you this because these were lessons that I only learned inside of my marriage; the signs were there, and I don't want you to ignore the signs and decide to marry someone who has issues with rage. As a dating woman, allow me to say that a man who is abusive will not always wait to marry you to begin vetting you for abuse. Understand that his being abusive in any way, shape, or form in the dating stages of your relationship is bold but happens more often than you think. Take his behavior as a sign from God. You could have made the biggest mistake of your life by staying with him! Either way, married or single, there is no way that you should be in that environment. For those of you who feel compelled to ensure that he gets help, I say get to safety and let that grown man be a grown man. He will be just fine. He has a father who loves him and wants to heal every deficiency that he is willing to surrender to him. Again, this is not your job.

One thing that God spoke into my situation very distinctly was that He was God and I was not! He said, "Lisa, if he wants Me and wants Me to change him, he will come to Me whether you intervene or not." I had to get to a place where I believed God because by remaining and trying to proctor him through the process, I was actually more of a hinderance because I was in God's way. I have to admit, at that time, God was not my source. I know He wasn't because if He was, I never would have put someone in His place. That is all abuse is—it is the enemy putting someone else in God's place in your life to cause such confusion that in some instances you can't hear God anymore. If you can't hear God, you can't fulfill your purpose, and that is the enemy's entire campaign.

But, I have come to serve notice on the devil that he can't have you. Get up, dry your tears, and get to safety. No one deserves to abuse you, not physically, not mentally, not spiritually, and not financially. No one has sacrificed what Jesus has sacrificed for you, and if He would not subject you to such tyranny, neither can anyone else—and I do mean anyone, not friends and not family. No has earned the right to abuse you! Remember, the person who can only find peace in tormenting others is himself tormented. That is a spirit, and it needs to be called out! You need to leave. No matter what your local church may have told you about God's ability to heal someone, He can do that no matter where YOU are. Do not accept it. Obviously, I am directing a lot of my comments to any woman who knows or may be an abused woman, but if you are an abused single woman, I plead with you. Get help! How dare someone lay a finger on you or try to break your spirit. It is never okay, love, and you don't have to take it anymore.

Let's Pray

Heavenly Father, I thank You for the singles who have read this and pray something has pricked their spirit to rethink what may be a bad decision. Lord, help them to see You as a God who loves them with everything You have. Take away all bad counsel, take away all feelings of shame, take away all perceptions of weakness, and declare to them that they are not weak because they reached out for help, but they are strong in You! Help them to be guided to relationships with real men of God. Men who lift their hands to worship You, who stretch their arms to serve Your people, and who have a healthy reverence for You and a fear of breaking Your heart.

God, help my sisters to handle themselves with care. It can be so scary to go through this and face the court of public opinion but help them to realize that those opinions are just another trick of the enemy to keep them in bondage. Make them strong in You. You said because we know Your name, You would deliver us, if we hold fast to You in love. Well, we love You with our whole hearts, and because we love You, You promised to protect us. You said we can just call and You would answer us and, Lord, we are calling on You.

Father, help every one of my sisters who may not even feel strong enough to leave. I bind any spirit of wasted time. I bind every soul tie that would hinder my sister from leaving a bad situation. Help her to stop replying to the texts and help her to stop answering the phone. Lord, help her to hear once and for all the truth and be set free. I bind any spirit that would say it has been too long to give up the relationship now.

Oh, God, You promised to be with us in trouble, You promised to honor us, and You promised to rescue us. Please, Father, satisfy us with long lives and show us Your salvation, for this day we declare that You are our dwelling place. We lift our souls, our hearts, and our prayers to You, oh Lord, our strength and our Redeemer. In the blood of the crucified Savior, we pray it is so! Amen.

At some point, we all have either been abused or know someone who has. If you need help, please contact The National Domestic Abuse Hotline at 1-800-799-7233. Phone lines are available 24/7/365. And if you need a prayer partner, my contact information is included at the end of this book. I love you, and you can do this.

CHAPTER

YOUR LIES

> *Do not be conformed to this world, but be transformed by the renewal of your mind, that by testing you may discern what is the will of God, what is good and acceptable and perfect.*
>
> **Romans 12:2 (ESV)**

The Problem

We have been lied to. We have been sold a false reality and have allowed those principles to be taken on as truth because of the people around us. We allow the opinions of other people to urge us to make important life decisions, forgetting that we are the ones that have to live with the decisions that we make. It has been ingrained in us from the beginning of time that in order to be a successful woman, we have to get married. There is no way we could possibly be fulfilled in our lives without the man of our dreams, right? He was the key. His money, his influence, and his fame were to be the jewels in our crown. We were groomed to be someone's better half. But is that really truth, or is that a standard passed down generation to generation? Is it even accurate?

And before you throw this book out of the window, I know that you are thinking, *Oh God! I am single, and it feels like I will be in this condition forever.* Listen to me, because I am about to drop a bomb that will leave you speechless. Are you ready? Here it goes: that path of thought is a lie. Being single will not kill you! Argh! I know you didn't want to hear that! But it is true. Being single will not kill you. You haven't heard of one death by single thus far, but wouldn't that be funny? I can hear it now! "Stop! Wait... woman down!", I can see everyone coming to rush in to stand over the body. Someone whispers, "What happened to her? How did she die?" Then they all shake their heads. "Girl, the single got her!"

I am laughing so hard right now, and of course I am joking, but I am also serious. We treat singleness like it is a terminal illness. We see all of the cute little couples at church and the selfies with the kissy faces all over social media, and we lose

66

our minds! Sweetheart! Stop. Single is not a disease. Quite the contrary, if you use the time wisely, singleness can be the most exhilarating and transforming time you will spend in your life. And if you are intentional and use it for purpose, then it can be some of the best years of your life.

Best believe I did not come to this realization easily, nor did I initially volunteer to be single. I admit there were very distinct things I enjoyed about being in a relationship, but something had to give, and God knew that there was more inside of me than I was allowing to surface. In some instances, it was the relationships that I was in that kept those giftings hidden and locked away. So, when God revealed this truth to me and placed me in a private suite for Him to be the only one with access to me, I had to face the fact that I had no idea why I had suppressed my gifts for so many years.

Trust me, I was not always this way. I can remember some seasons where God had to drag me through certain stages of singleness kicking and screaming, but He got me through it. He just didn't want me to die. Yes, I said die. In some senses, I was already dead. I was walking through life as a corpse. No sign of purpose, no sign of life. Just drifting through the years, supporting someone else, and if I am honest, my purpose was the last thing I was concerned with. I felt like a zombie; I knew that there was more inside me but had no idea how to bring it out. Then the enemy told me things like, "You have squandered your gifts—it is too late for you!" And I believed him, so I drifted even further away from the will of God. But trust me, this is yet another lie!

At the time, I was so buried in my own reality that I thought a relationship was what I needed to make it all better. Sometimes we try to fix ourselves by adding a person to our mess, but if we mess around and tie ourselves to the wrong person, it can be fatal. "Fatal" may feel like a stretch to some of you, but trust me, marrying the wrong person can mean death to your dreams, death to your goals, or worse—death to your purpose. What lies have you believed? Do you believe you are not smart enough? Not good enough? Have you bought into the lie that a man is going to come in and fix the mess you've made? We must stop this.

Allow me to share some truth with you and cut the shackles of dishonesty that the enemy has placed on you. You need God. He is the answer to the life you want. Sometimes in the body of Christ, when women speak this way, the impression becomes that I am a feminist and I am diminishing the impact of the order that God has set forth in the home. That is a lie. In Genesis 2:18 (ESV), God told us very clearly what role we are to play in the home. It says, "The LORD God said, 'It is not good for the man to be alone. I will make a helper suitable for him.'" Your role is to be a helper—and not just any helper, but one that is suitable for your husband.

While you are hidden, you should be asking God one question: "Lord, am I suitable for the man I am asking you to bless me with?" If you ask God that question, He will answer you. And when you ask Him to posture you in a way that you can be an acceptable mate, He will begin to expose every lie the enemy has fed you. He is a faithful and loving God and He wants His best for you, but His best will come at the price of your complete surrender.

I submit to you that a good reason we take on the lies of the world as truth is because the lies are easier to deal with. If I can lay up in a dirty house with bad credit and believe that God is going to send a man to clean it all up, then of course I am going to believe the lie. The lie is more comfortable; the lie doesn't require any change on my part. As you know, change, by definition, is uncomfortable. But that is not what God asks of you. What God is wanting to do in this time is grow you, and you can't do that if you remain snuggled up with the lies the enemy has told you. Resolve in your spirit that you will walk in truth today and spend time with God, devising an action plan to root out every lie the devil has planted in you and replacing it with God's truth.

What Happened to Us?

We are women of the twenty-first century. We have progressed emotionally, financially, and professionally, so it escapes me why the issue of waiting still paralyzes us. I think it is because we have bought into man's idea of timelines. It's like we came out of utero with a schedule. From the day we were born, we are groomed to think about starting a family, and it just isn't like that for men.

When a baby girl is born, what is the first toy a little girl gets? Usually a doll and a stroller, a kitchen set, or Barbies with the perfect little house and perfect little Ken. Our entire lives, parenthood and family are modeled for us and almost ingrained into who we are. Again, there is nothing wrong with being a wife. I am just saying that boys' first gifts are usually something like firetrucks, and I don't see the media shoving that idea down men's throats.

We have all seen the movie where the successful, beautiful thirtysomething single woman is attending a family dinner and inevitably has to discuss why she isn't married yet. No one is confronting the thirtysomething single man at the table for never becoming a fireman; in fact, they are encouraging him to take his time and play the field. Meanwhile, we are the ones waiting for men like him to get it together. We are waiting for men (some, not all) who have never been groomed to be heads of their household to finish playing the field, so we can marry them.

Do you see the point of contention between the sexes from the very beginning? We are taught two very different things, and the difficult part is we need each other in order to move either of these narratives ahead. If we are going to get married like we were trained to do, we need him. And if he is going to play the field and sow his wild oats, he needs us. So, we find ourselves in relationships, and sometimes we are both walking in with very different ideas of what the finish line looks like.

Of course, this is not new to you. You know how hard it is to find a mate that is worthwhile. But in defense of men, there are some women, not all, that believe they can circumvent the process by being a temporary playmate because they think they will end up as a wife. But, love, if he wants to play, a playmate is all you are now and all you will ever be. Your position plays into his false belief system that part of maturing is to play for a while and then get serious with his real woman. Think about it. How many booty calls do you think evolve into long-term relationships? I can answer that—MAYBE one out of fifty and, who knows, maybe you are the one. I doubt it, but we can hope, right?

Even if you are, it is likely that it will be years before he decides to settle for you, and by then you have wasted your best years as a toy for a boy rather than as a mate for a man. I know this isn't what you want to hear, but I love you enough to ask you to consider what I am saying. Haven't you tried it your way? Is it working? If not, then we have to make some changes. I was no different. I thought getting married would clean up the huge mess I had made of my dating life so, in my haste, I married someone who demonstrated that he was still in a season of playing. Funny how we think marriage is a cure-all—it's not. If you marry someone who is a lifelong player, a wedding ring doesn't change the type of man he has decided to be, and trust me, no woman can make a man mature. That is between God and him. I firmly believe that is why God made him first, so that he would always know that God expected to be first in his life.

So, let's get it over with. Let's have the inevitable conversation because, ladies, we need some truth. The enemy is using lies to keep us in this crazy place, and we just can't stay here. We can't afford to…

Sin

My old pastor used to say, "Sin takes you further than you want to go and keeps you longer than you want to stay." Isn't that the truth? But there is a huge misconception about sin. Yes, sin is real. We are in progressive times where we hear so many different descriptions and definitions of what sin is, but when all is said and done, sin is sin—and God does not like it. Do not let this constant message of acceptance and grace fool you. God has not changed, and He is not soft. We may have changed the Word of God so that it can be more palatable, but that is what we as a society have done to the Word, not what God has spoken in the Word.

I remember speaking with a friend of mine and listening to them rationalize the reason that sin was okay. We were speaking about sex outside of marriage, and she went on and on about how God knows that we are going to sin and that was why He sent Jesus to die so that He would cover it. I remember being so upset because I could tell that she really believed that there was no need to change certain things about her life because God would just forgive her anyway.

Again, this is a lie from the enemy, and a huge trap. Take a closer look at Romans 6:1-2 (ESV) "Well then, should we keep on sinning so that God can show us more and more of his wonderful grace? Of course not! Since we have died to sin, how can we continue to live in it?"

First, look at what this scripture says. In layman's terms, it says just because God has sent Christ to die for us, does not mean that we are to continue to sin. How many times have you heard someone say, "Well, I sinned, but God knows my heart"? That statement should scare you beyond belief. Not because it isn't true, but because it *is* true. God *does* know your heart. He knows your heart and your mind and your body. He knows every time you ask for forgiveness and aren't really sorry. He knows every time you plan to sin, and He is there anyway. So, let me ask you this: how many times can I slap you in your face and apologize for it before you realize that I am not really sorry? Now imagine an omnipresent God who knows you better than you know yourself. Do you really want to continue to try and deceive yourself into thinking that He doesn't know when you aren't genuinely trying to correct your behavior?

Sisters, we have it wrong! Misappropriation of grace is just that. God knows when a drug addict is compelled to use, and He is there with no judgement and accepts them and invites them back to Him. God knows when you truly want to change and just can't seem to, but make no mistake that the same God knows when you are attempting to game the system; He is not fooled. I would invite you to read Romans 6 at length in your private time; it will change your view of sin and remind you of what you are doing to the heart of God when you volunteer to live in a way unpleasing to Him.

Sex

I know you knew it was coming, so let's talk about sex! We all love sex. Sex was made to be good, hence the reason we love it so much! I am going to encourage you to have sex. Yes, I am going to encourage you to have as much sex as you can possibly have—just don't have it unprotected. I can see the side eyes already. *What did she say?!* No doubt, every single reading this book has thrown it against a wall, but please hear me out. I want you to enjoy sex as God intended—fully protected by Him. No, I am not referencing condoms or birth control. I am referring to sex inside the bonds of marriage. Yes, God created sex for marriage, and He did it that way for a reason. Words can't express how difficult it was to accept this in my life. I was ready to walk away from a lot of things when I got a divorce, but sex was not one of them until the Holy Spirit dropped this on me. Get ready for some truth. Are you ready? Go get some water. Trust me, you will need it for this one.

When you choose to have sex outside the bonds of marriage, you are stealing from God! BOOM! Any sexual act outside of marriage is the equivalent of going through your mother's purse and taking what she probably intended for you to have anyway. I can already hear the heavy gasps and deep sighs. Is this another book touting abstinence like it is as easy as changing a blouse? Well, yes and no! Yes, I am going to tell you that God requires abstinence, and if you are honest with yourself, for the level of blessing you want in a relationship, you are requiring it as well. No, I am not going to pretend that it is going to be easy. Nobody knows better than me how hard it can be to say no to something that you like. Especially when you have already had it. So, accept that this is going to be a challenge. Buckle up and prepare. But I promise you this: you will not die.

During my time as a Christian single, of course I have been given the opportunity to have sex outside of marriage. Consequently, on my journey to abstinence (and it was a journey), I have had a couple of slip-ups. Before rededicating my body to God, I remember looking back on the last sexual experience I had and being so disgusted. Not just disgusted with the man but also disgusted with myself. But it wasn't the sex that disgusted me, per se. It was this new feeling that I had never felt before. It was weird. For the first time, I was seriously convicted and ashamed for indulging in behavior that disappointed God. It was surreal. Never in my life had I felt like I could actually feel the pain I was inflicting on God by sinning against Him. But one thing was for sure—whatever the feeling, I did not like it.

I vowed from that moment on to devote myself to keeping my temple pure before Him, and though it has been a journey, I am proud to say I am still abstinent. I don't share these things with you to discourage you or to make you feel like I am exalting myself because this is something that I have devoted myself to. Quite the opposite, actually. I am writing this to let you know that it is possible. You can live your life for God and still feel fulfilled. Before you jump off the deep end and start thinking that I am suggesting that you will never desire sex again until God sends you your man, let me stop you and say that in the beginning, these loins were on fire. I am not saying that you are not going to have some hard nights. What I am saying is that the God you serve is more than able to help you survive what may be one of the most trying tests of your flesh.

Think about it. This is not new; a lot of people in the Bible who did great things had SEX problems. Don't believe me? Think about King David. He was selected by God when he was only a boy. He defeated Goliath and then married the daughter of King Saul. He won many battles and became a great king. But he also saw a woman, Bathsheba, and he wanted her so badly that he was willing to kill to have her. One night he was walking the rooftop of his palace and saw her bathing. He was so smitten with her that he sent word for her to be brought to the palace. He slept with her and then she became pregnant; when he could not cover it up, he ultimately arranged the death of her husband. I would consider that a sex problem.

Look at his son Solomon, who had 700 wives and 300 concubines, good Lord! How did the man walk? Anyway, even though he had all of those women, this was still the same man who had the wisdom to ask God for the right things. In 1 Kings 3:11–12 (NIV), God says to Solomon, "'Since you have asked for this and not for long life or wealth for yourself, nor have asked for the death of your enemies but for discernment in administering justice, I will do what you have asked. I will give you a wise and discerning heart, so that there will never have been anyone like you, nor will there ever be.'" Look at the favor of God on his life. This was the wisest man on earth. Yet he still craved women, and it was the love for strange women that distanced him from God. I would say that is a major SEX problem.

By all accounts, sex problems are really just issues with self-control. We allow our flesh to dictate our actions, and then we are knocked off kilter. Self-control is a necessary component of any journey with God; it is an imperative. But God never puts us in a circumstance that we cannot survive. In 1 Corinthians 10:13 (NIV), it says, "No temptation has overtaken you except what is common to mankind. And God is faithful; he will not let you be tempted beyond what you can bear. But when you are tempted, he will also provide a way out so that you can endure it." God knows that we will be tempted. He desires for us to seek

Him in those moments. Are you tempted? Do you want to have sex? Of course you do, but you have to weigh whether or not it is worth it. What will you lose if you can't control your flesh? What will you gain? A child? A disease? A bad reputation? A broken heart? These are all factors that we have to consider when we knowingly decide to sin against God.

There is a scripture that is used a lot in the church, and it is also one of my favorites. It says: "Now to Him who is able to do exceedingly abundantly above all that we ask or think, according to the power that works in us, to Him be glory in the church by Christ Jesus to all generations, forever and ever. Amen" (Ephesians 3:20–21, NKJV). We use that scripture when we discuss the blessing of God. We get so excited and we laugh, we jump, we shout, and of course we high-five a neighbor forty-seven times when we hear it, because of how it makes us feel about the blessing of God, but I submit to you that if we are to take that perspective and truly hold to it, then that same scripture should be the one anchoring us to a life of holiness. If He is truly able to do "exceedingly" (to a great extent) and "abundantly" (in large quantities) above all or everything we can ask or think, then there should be some reverential fear when we knowingly disobey God. And let's not forget, according to the power that works in us, we are learning more and more every day what God has placed on the inside of us. If this statement is true, then when we make the decision to live outside of the will of God, we truly have no idea what level the consequence will be on. We think we know, but we have no idea.

Do you know how powerful you are? If you do, then you also know that with great power comes great responsibility. You have to equip yourself for all you will go through on this journey of waiting for the right one. I wish I could tell you that there will not be times where you will be tempted to settle. You will… but don't. Do not allow yourself to be bullied into doing what displeases God. Let me prepare you, because the enemy is a cunning adversary who knows just what you like. He is not going to send you someone who isn't what you want. On the contrary, he may send you a "man of God" who can preach the Word up one side and down the other, but the truth is, a real man of God will do his absolute best to preserve your purity because he is in it for the long haul.

Carnal men will attempt to tell you that this is an area they have not surrendered to God. I remember a gentleman telling me that I needed to be more compassionate for men who have not attained that level of understanding in that area. I laughed because it is a lie. Listen, when God has delivered you from something, no matter what it is, you don't shrink back to what He has delivered you from to appease someone else. If they are not there, pray for them, but don't undo what God has cultivated in you so that someone who may be temporary will be happy. You have worked hard to get to that place with God, and you have made the sacrifices and learned the hard lessons. Don't downplay that. Stand in your beliefs, and God will honor you.

Abstinence is about trust in God, period. Every time you are tempted, remind yourself that there are no degrees to trusting God. You either trust Him or you don't. If your sent man trusts in God, then waiting for you won't be that much of a sacrifice because he is believing God for something as well. His being abstinent has nothing to do with you as much as it has to do with his relationship with God. The man God has for you will desire to please Him with his whole heart, and by doing everything in his power to crucify his flesh, he lives a life holy unto God. He has a mandate on his life and can recognize the same in you. The man God has for you guards his anointing and is equally concerned about yours, so he needs to let you know who he is in Christ because if he is not the man for you, then he is a danger to you and you need to move on. The man God has for you deserves for you to protect his space until his arrival; you should not be filling it up with casual encounters and time wasters. You must set the expectation, and if he will not follow suit, then God has better for you.

Masturbation

I know some of you cringed when you saw that word, but we have to unpack all of this if we are to prosper in our singleness. Another lie the enemy has told us is that masturbation is acceptable because it involves only you. Let's clear this up: masturbation is a sin. Period. We try to have these loopholes to hacking abstinence, but the truth is that it is sin! I have actually had women in the church suggest to me that I should go to a sex shop to purchase toys to keep me holy until my husband arrives. Imagine that—toys to keep you holy! Listen, it is the same thing. It is a kind of sex. Abstinence from sexual behavior means all kinds of sexual behavior. Whether you want to acknowledge it or not, it is a sin.

How do I know? The Bible often speaks on lust. How can you masturbate without lust? You cannot be lying in a bed and pleasing yourself to climax without a single thought in your head to drive the feeling. If you think it, you are lusting, and lusting is a sin. Jesus even said you don't even have to commit adultery; you can just look at the woman or man lustfully, and if you do, you have already committed adultery in your heart.

So why do we do it? Why are we so comfortable compartmentalizing certain areas of our lives and only giving the Holy Spirit access to the parts we want Him to have? As a rule, you should not be doing anything that you can't invite the Holy Spirit to witness. God is there. You acknowledge that He is, and you know that He sees everything, so what makes this act any different? There has got to be a time when you can hear people in leadership say something that you know is not truth and make the decision to get your Bible and study for yourself. God is not going to accept an excuse of, "Well, my pastor said it was okay and he is my leader, so I did it." It won't give you a pass; if anything, both you and your pastor will be found guilty.

Again, this is us getting better and living in a way that pleases God in all areas of our singleness. I think you can agree that there are plenty of things God has given us to do in this walk that would be classified as difficult. If it was simple, then everyone would do it. But you have it in you, and you can get through this—I know you can.

Here are some scriptures from the ESV for your study time:

- "For all that is in the world—the desires of the flesh and the desires of the eyes and pride in possessions—is not from the Father but is from the world" (1 John 2:16).

- "But I say, walk by the Spirit, and you will not gratify the desires of the flesh" (Galatians 5:16).

- "So, flee youthful passions and pursue righteousness, faith, love, and peace, along with those who call on the Lord from a pure heart" (2 Timothy 2:22).

- "Put to death therefore what is earthly in you: sexual immorality, impurity, passion, evil desire, and covetousness, which is idolatry" (Colossians 3:5).

Do We Even Know What We Want?

Another lie we have been told is that we do not know what we want. I do not believe that the majority of the women looking to be found by someone are unaware of what they want. If this were true, they would not be able to articulate it so well to each other. I believe the opposite is true. I believe that women know exactly what they want. Yes, we do. The problem is that when no candidates around us look like what we want, we historically settle and try to turn whatever option is available into what we want. Huge mistake! Then we cry and we complain that we just can't believe that we ended up in that situation. I am telling you from my own experience. I should have ventured to write children's books because I created fairy tale after fairy tale with many a frog, expecting happily-ever-after instead of just accepting it for what it truly was.

Listen, sis, do not downgrade your vision based on the options available. You must be brave enough to wait. Don't try to make something that looks nothing like what you are believing God for, into what you want. God has someone fit for you, and you will need to be willing to wait on Him to send him. Abandoning your desire and accepting whatever someone is willing to give you will do nothing but make you resentful. You deserve more, and God has it for you.

So to recap, yes, you can get your life together. You do not need a man to do it for you. You should add to him and he should add to you—and from a healthy place, not a place of scarcity. You do not have to settle for being someone's playmate, and you really don't want to be with a man who is content to take all of the benefits that only your husband should have access to anyway. Abstinence is not going to kill you, nor will it be forever. Once you get married, you can have all of the sex you want. In the meantime, masturbation is not the way—you can wait without gaming the system. You do know what you want, and you do have options, so just wait until the correct one presents itself. Finally, you have a real God who loves you and is excited about giving you His very best. Do the same for Him.

Let's Pray

Heavenly Father, I ask You now to touch the sisters reading this. Help them to unpack all of the lies that they have told themselves to survive. Lord, You are a God of truth, and we only prosper in You when we operate in truth. So, Lord, reveal to us the areas where we have settled to believe you for less than we should.

Father, we want to please You. Keep us pure and help us to hold up a standard. Keep our minds, our bodies, and our spirits. Lord, it is not easy to abstain from sex when the world has bought into the idea that abstinence is an old-fashioned idea but, Lord, remind us that we are to look to You. The world cannot teach us to be women of God—that is for You to do. Father, teach us self-control. Help us in moments when we are confident that we will fall and be all we need. We ask all of these things through You. Amen.

CHAPTER 4

YOUR RELATIONSHIPS

> *For I know the plans I have for you, declares the*
> *Lord, plans for welfare and not for evil, to give you a*
> *future and a hope.*
>
> *Jeremiah 29:11 (ESV)*

Your Relationship with God

It is so easy to find ourselves busy with just living life. Our jobs are demanding, our lives are filled with obligation, and we, as women, are pulled in so many directions. I can tell you that I have been serving God for the majority of my life, and only recently have I become aware of how crucial my quality time is with Him.

In 2012, I found myself in one of the most difficult seasons of my life. I was walking through what I would consider a season of humiliation, and to add insult to injury, I had this beautiful little girl depending on her mommy for all of the answers. If you are not a parent, you probably don't understand the pressures that come with guiding the life of another human being, but it is tough, and being a single parent made it even more difficult. How could I be responsible for another human life when I was uncertain about what to do with my own life?

I remember watching as this life I thought I had just deteriorated right in front of my eyes. There is nothing worse than thinking you have control over something and realizing that it really has control over you. I knew it was a result of my poor decision-making, and it sickened me. I did everything in my power to control appearances. I tried to paint a positive picture of everything in my life, but I did a poor job of actually living the life I pretended to love. If I am honest, I hated my life. I hated myself and felt truly alone because I had muted God in an attempt to have what I wanted instead of what He wanted to give me. I hated what I had become, and I hated that I had allowed the enemy access to my life on any level. Which is exactly what I did.

You see, when you are disobedient to God, you give the enemy an access-granted pass to meddle in your life, and before you know it, you are so far away from God that you aren't quite certain about anything anymore. I used to lie in bed and wonder how I would face the world after suffering such humiliation. I was so disillusioned with everything. I didn't want to go back to church. I disconnected from friends. I realized people's true heart for me, and it wasn't always good. In fact, it became clear where I landed on people's priority list. I was at my lowest. I wasn't even a person anymore; I had become mere conversation—something for people to discuss and be entertained by. It was all too overwhelming for me to handle.

In hindsight, I know that God allowed everything to happen the way it did for a reason, and I am so grateful that He did. It forced me to face some bitter truths that I had been masking for a long time, and it made me develop my relationship with Him. A personal relationship with God is essential because there will be times when the noise of life is blaring in your ears, and your eyes will be so heavy with tears that you can't bear to breathe. Have you ever been there? There have been times in my life where something as simple as breathing felt like physical pain. A new moment of agony accompanied every breath because I couldn't believe I had allowed myself to get in the position I was in. The wounds I carried were so burdensome that I was sure I would collapse under the pressure. Yet somehow in the midst of my distress, God was there.

I remember lying on the floor and lamenting that everyone who was supposed to care about me was gone. I was having a pretty successful pity party, if I do say so myself. I remember being ashamed and telling God I needed Him to send someone to comfort me. I had become so accustomed to looking to people for comfort that I had actually asked Him to help me by sending someone to help instead of crying, "Lord, please help me." Isn't that crazy? I can't recall exactly how it happened. I don't know when I became so dependent on people, but I do remember spending a night of tears and wailing, asking God how He could allow me to lose everything. My friends were gone, my marriage was over, and even my child was going through incredible pain. I couldn't find the words. I could barely breathe, let alone speak, but I managed to ask Him, "God… where were you? What were you doing when I was making a mess of my life?" Then, very quietly, very deliberately, I heard, "I was there."

I was in shock because it was the first time that I had a solid confidence that the voice I heard was God. And listen, I don't care how sad you are. When you hear voices and you know that you are in the house alone, that perks you right up! It wasn't a big, long production—just nine little words that would change my life forever. He said, "I was there then, and I am here now." I would love to tell you that in that moment, I immediately changed my relationship with God and pressed in to hearing His voice often, but I didn't. I was still so very hurt that the hurt was all I could hear consistently, but our God is so patient! He took His time with me. In my obedience and willingness to listen to

Him when He was speaking, He walked me through those tough seasons of grief, embarrassment, and frustration.

Sometimes in our journey, we wonder if God is speaking to us. The answer is yes. In fact, God never stops speaking, but we have to be intentional about making time to listen to Him. I only wish I would have listened to God without needing to experience the turmoil that drove me to my face. Sometimes the only time we can see God is when the world has driven our face into the pavement, and we have no choice but to incline our ears to His will concerning us. I used to wonder why God didn't provide burning-bush moments for me. If He wanted to speak to me so badly, why didn't He just set my balcony on fire or something? I certainly would have appreciated a megaphone or something like that to shake me and get me to realize what I was doing to myself, but God isn't that way. Not anymore. Now, because of His extreme love for us, He desires a personal, one-on-one relationship, and that requires cultivating.

I remember when I was newly divorced, I thought I was going to jump straight into the dating pool. I mean, I was single, right? At the time, the only prerequisite for dating me was being single and sane. Boy, was I ill-informed! Anyway, in an attempt to get my life together, I began this pattern of waking up in the morning to talk with God. No matter what I had going on, I made it my business to talk to HIM. I had become intentional about communicating with Him consistently, and I was very proud of the progress we were making.

Well, I was all in for a good three months, and then I started noticing that my sleep was starting to get really good to me right around the time I would normally be waking up. Before I knew it, I was sleeping in and sometimes forgetting to speak with God altogether. I kind of put myself on my own schedule. But when you have conditioned yourself to speak with God consistently and then a period of time passes without that quality time, it sticks out like a sore thumb.

I began to get convicted so the next morning, I decided to wake up early and have my time with God. As per usual, I was writing in my journal. On this particular day, I was writing about my fear of making another mistake in relationships, and God said, "You aren't going to date for a while. You need to spend some time getting to know yourself."

Keep in mind that at that time, I was in my mid-thirties and I thought, *How can You tell me I don't know myself?*

I am sure you can imagine my frustration, and in true God form, a small voice, clear as a bell, said, "Because you don't know Me yet."

Wow! I thought. *I don't know you? I have been baptized and saved my whole life. I don't know you?*

He said, "No, you don't." I remember feeling so sad, but God is so loving, He reminded me of all of the twisted belief systems I had because of the incomplete Gospel I was raised on. He said very clearly, "When you truly know Me, you will recognize My character in others, and you won't have to be afraid."

It was hard to accept His instruction, but He was so right. I had to accept that I had a skewed view of God. The God I was introduced to had tons of blurred lines and dogmatic doctrine. The God I grew up on only cared about the plan of salvation but not my everyday needs. The God I knew was more of a figurehead to be admired, but there was no evidence of transformation in the lives of those around me. As I think back, I know where my view of God took a turn for the worse. I had always been taught to view God as a father, and that didn't work for me because I didn't truly know what a healthy father-daughter relationship looked like. I viewed God the Father the way I viewed my biological father—mean and abusive.

Sisters, we are limited by our perception, and if our view of God is skewed, then everything else is an optical illusion. For example, when you enter a funhouse at a local fair, there are some mirrors that make you appear really big while others make you appear really skinny. A life without a clear view of who God is, is like living in a funhouse. Your perception is warped and twisted, so therefore your ideologies are the same.

I can't tell you of a better day than the day God took me off the market. Some of you are off the market right now and don't even realize it because you haven't taken the time to ask God if you are ready for everything you are asking Him to send you. This is a time to know Him and spend time with Him and Him only. He faithfully took me through every season—good, bad, and ugly. I was broken, an emotional wreck. I had so many scars, I thought healing would take forever, but He comforted me. I wanted to change my career, and He opened every door. I wanted to see Him move in the life of my child, and He mended her broken heart and made her a warrior for Him. He restored so much more to me in this life than I ever imagined possible, but I firmly believe that none of this would have happened if I wasn't intentional about being in His presence, spending time with HIM and learning His character.

Do you know God? Has He shown Himself to you? Please note that I am not asking if you go to church. Going to church doesn't mean you know God; it means you have some time blocked out on your calendar. In this day and age, it can be easy to mistake acquaintance with real relationship. We see it every day—just because we know something about someone or we have become familiar with them, we think we know them. Never settle for being casually acquainted with God because only by living day by day in fellowship with HIM will you truly know Him. Truly knowing Him is an intimate process, and it must be cultivated. Knowing Him is to want to spend time with Him, even if no one else is there. To want to know Him is to be in His presence daily and to submit all the events of that day to Him. As you do this, you will begin to know yourself.

I did not truly know how capable I was of loving myself, flaws and all, until I fell in love with God. His presence is breathtaking; it's like walking on the beach and seeing the sunrise for the first time, but you get to witness that newness every day. Like Lamentations 3:22–23 (ESV) says: "The steadfast love of the Lord never ceases; his mercies never come to an end; they are new every morning; great is your faithfulness."

Now I know I have to be careful because people will assume that because I am saying how beautiful the presence of God is, I am insinuating that I must never have any problems. Not true. However, I can say that when the walls are caving in around me and the worries and cares of this life try to suffocate me and silence my praise, it feels like I am protected and unfazed by what is going on around me. If you don't believe me, you should try it. Try praying to God and pressing into Him. I promise you will notice the difference in how you react to the world around you. Conversely, attempt to take a week to try things on your own. I guarantee you, you will be more anxious, overwhelmed, discouraged, and frustrated, primarily because lightening your load is what He does for His children.

In His Word, he says His yoke is easy and His burdens are light. I know people always refer to the yoke as an instrument around the neck of an ox to help him pull a plow, but this scripture is to remind you that you are not the ox—you are the farmer sitting on the porch, drinking lemonade, while all of your needs are being met. Why? Because for God it isn't a yoke at all. It is light for Him; He doesn't have to move an inch to change your situation. But when you decide to put that yoke on your shoulders, you will inevitably buckle under the pressure because you were not built to carry it. Press into God and let Him carry your heavy load.

If you are a single and discouraged by the desire in your heart to marry, take inventory. What do you need to surrender to God? What can the Lord take off your plate? How can He make you whole? He knows you. He knows your needs, and He plans to address the desires of your heart. He just needs you to get to know Him before He turns you loose on the world.

Your Relationships with Friends and Family

Two are better than one, because they have a good reward for their toil. For if they fall, one will lift up his fellow. But woe to him who is alone when he falls and has not another to lift him up! Again, if two lie together, they keep warm, but how can one keep warm alone? And though a man might prevail against one who is alone, two will withstand him—a threefold cord is not quickly broken.

Ecclesiastes 4:9–12 (ESV)

Friends

I used to be one of those women that had no female friends. I made excuses as to why I could never thrive in those types of friendships. For the longest time, I just preferred to hang out with men; they were so much easier to deal with than women— or so I thought, until I realized that men gossiped just as much as women. It was a very weird realization for me to come to, and I was sure that I was destined to walk through this life alone.

Then one day, as I was feeling really sorry for myself, God reprimanded me. He reminded me that I was not being pure. He spurred me to reexamine why I wanted friends in the first place; after a closer look, I noticed that my motives for cultivating friendships really revolved around my need to be needed, not a desire to be the best friend I could be. I found that because I came from a place of impure motives, I attached myself to people with impure motives. I needed to be needed, and they needed someone to use. I jumped at the opportunity to do anything they needed, and then when they misused me, I turned victim quick! Suddenly I was lamenting about how unfair their treatment of me was and held on to every bit of hurt they doled out.

When God finally got tired of hearing me cry and ask Him to heal my heart, He reminded me that I was called to be a steward, not just of my resources but of my time, talents and, yes, relationships. He reminded me that I allowed a lot of the opportunities for the hurt that I experienced, and He also showed me times when I was not the nicest person to be friends with either. You see, I was very self-critical, and sometimes I was critical of others as well. I was not only critical, but in some cases, I was very selfish. I thought about my needs and would be so consumed by what was happening to me that I would not begin to consider the fact that my friends had things happening to them as well. I was very comfortable being a victim in my relationships, and I often expected people to rescue me. But Jesus is my Savior, right? Isn't He yours? So how can you have the expectation that people are to sacrifice everything for you? You see? Faulty belief systems!

I truly believe that a lot of us do not thrive in our relationships because we do not realize that we are unprepared to do what it takes to have one. I came to my friendships and relationships with a list of everything they could do for me, giving no consideration of what I would have to contribute. I would do way too much and then be mad when it wasn't appreciated. God had to change that. So, what did I do? I prayed, and I asked God for the first time in my life to be my rescuer. I stopped judging. Well, I try—it is a daily journey to remind myself that I have not arrived, but with God's help, I can keep that internal judge and jury covered and gagged by the blood of Jesus!

I also asked God to show me what healthy friendships looked like and to send them to me. I know it is tempting to desire a bunch of people who will hang out with you and call you all of the time, but in this season, you may as well prepare to be looked over for the hangouts. You are in a season of making, so there will be days when your phone does not ring, and you won't be invited to events. Allow that to be okay.

Become okay with being ignored and overlooked; it is for a purpose. View it as a blessing in disguise, and as you avail yourself to God, you will notice that one by one, He sends the right people to pour into you at the right time. He knows what you need, so while He spends this time with you, ask Him to grace you with friendships that bring Him glory.

Spend time cultivating your friendship skills. If you see a fellow sister in Christ, smile at her! What are you so mad about? You are not in competition with each other! How are you blessed, highly favored, and rude? It is okay to be kind. Say hello, and if you speak to someone and that person can't reciprocate, then pray for their insecurity. You are in a season now where you are becoming a complete woman of God. This is the time for Him to perfect that which is concerning you. Pour out your heart to Him. Tell Him that you need Him to teach you to be a friend and then be one. I guarantee that as you hone your skills in extending friendship and kindness, it will prepare you for the promise God has for you all the more.

Family

As for family, I was pretty much in the same boat. As the black sheep, I always felt like an outsider. I never felt good enough, and trust me, no one can break you down like your family. When I was in some of the darkest seasons of my life, I faced them alone, and I was really frustrated that they were not there for me. Then I had to realize that, again, I had to forgive and move on with my life. Family is a very complex thing; it is a group of people that is given to you by blood, sometimes to make you stronger. You will not always agree, and you will not always feel like you have been treated fairly, but when all is said and done, God has given you this family for a reason.

I used to be very resentful of other people who had close-knit families that were together all of the time and celebrated each other's differences. I used to be frustrated that my family wasn't that way. Thank God for my siblings and their acceptance of me; they have always been pretty loving toward me, but my extended family in some ways was very difficult. Primarily because they fought all of the time. I could not understand where all of the anger came from. They just always seemed mad. But when God brought me to a hidden place, He separated me from them just enough to hear and understand all of their individual struggles and stories.

If you have family members that you really don't know, I invite you to reach out and get an understanding, and don't try to have them help you understand. Ask God. Realize that there are some family members that you just won't mesh with, and that is okay. Just because you share blood doesn't mean you should share space. I love every member of my family, but I have accepted that we are not all the same—and I am okay with that. If anything, those differences are what make my family so beautiful, and I have noticed that if there is something you feel is missing in your life, God will send someone to fill in the blanks.

In my case, He sent tons of pseudo family members to step in and love me when I needed them. Acceptance begins with realizing where you falter, and there are times where we, as family, are not doing our part. In my case, I held my family to this unattainable expectation, and in actuality I knew that they would never be able to live up to it. If you are a member of a family that is filled with people that don't know how to be family, accept that they do not know and move on. Let them off the hook, because when you meet someone who loves you, when he marries you, he marries them. He needs to see a woman who can love completely and, yes, that means loving her family as well.

One of my biggest issues was feeling that no matter what I did, they were determined to remind me of my failures. Do you have family like that? I have a couple of family members that tell the same exact story about me at every family function. I mean, this event happened when I was seven, but they will tell it from the beginning as if I have never heard it before, over and over again. It used to infuriate me. Then one day God reminded me that I was putting too much faith in my family. They are human! He reminded me that even Jesus felt forgotten by His family. Mark 6:4 (NIV) says: "Jesus said to them, 'A prophet is not without honor except in his own town, among his relatives and in his own home.'" Jesus had done miracles; thousands had seen signs and wonders, and He still had that one family member that had to be negative. Can you imagine that? I can hear it now: "Oh yeah, I heard He raised someone from the dead, but I have known him his whole life, He ain't nobody, once he tripped on his sandals walking down a dirt road!" Really? Why do people feel the need to constantly diminish someone back to their perception of them?

The short answer is because if they acknowledge your progress, they must then acknowledge that they haven't been brave enough to make progress themselves. It truly has nothing to do with you. Some people will love you but never like you while some people will embrace you and find you a joy to be around. Either way, their shots at you have very little to do with you and everything to do with what they are not happy with in their own lives. Be you! Take the shots and move on. You can't do anything about the favor of God on your life, and you certainly do not serve God's positive purpose by shrinking back and acting like He has not blessed you. If God has advanced you, wear it proudly. You being you only upsets those who are uncomfortable with the decisions they have made. Don't get offended when people try to keep you in a certain place in their lives. Their reaction is based on fear! They know that if they allow you to move out of that position, it will inadvertently challenge them to move out of the position they themselves are stuck in, and they may not be ready to do that. Let me caution you to remember that your family loves you, but they can only love you from where they are.

Family is so important, but nonetheless, they are relationships. For every negative family relationship I have experienced, God has given me a positive one. For every family member that speaks negatively of me, I have ten family members that are cheering me on. The family relationship requires love and acceptance. You may not always agree, and you may never hang out. That is okay, but love and pray for them, and ask God to change your heart to be one that receives and gives love with no expectations. Set boundaries, and when they are crossed, remove yourself from the toxic situation. If there is hurt there, apologize, but move on. Don't give the enemy a foothold to cause division in your family. Sometimes the best way to keep a family together is to keep them apart. However, never stop praying for your family. You may not be able to unite them, but you can do your part to heal. If everyone takes ownership of their contributions to the family dynamic, then you should be well on your way to great relationships!

Let's Pray

Heavenly Father, thank You for my friends and my family. I repent to You for every time I was not what I needed to be. I ask You to show me every instance where I chose to be the root of division instead of an olive branch for peace. Lord, if I have not been the type of friend, sister, niece, daughter, or cousin that

I should have been, I ask You to improve me and incline my ear to hear Your voice. I have been wrong, and I am sorry. I have been more concerned about being right than being pleasing, and I ask for Your repentance now. Lord, bind us closer so that we can get to know You for real and serve Your kingdom to bring You glory.

Heal every hurt now, Lord. I release every form of anger, mental or physical abuse, hurt, disappointment, deception, and dishonesty, and I put on Your love, joy, peace, patience, kindness, goodness, faithfulness, gentleness, and self-control. There is no one like You on all the earth, and I vow to walk pleasing to You, and ask Your healing in these relationships now, in Jesus's name. Amen.

CHAPTER

YOUR CHARACTER

The integrity of the upright guides them, but the
crookedness of the treacherous destroys them.

Proverbs 11:3 (ESV)

What do people know about you? What is the one thing that people would say about you consistently? Would they talk about how dependable you are? Would they boast about your heart for God and His people? How many people would give rave reviews about you?

If you have no idea what others would say about you, chances are that you have not lived in a way that displays good character. Of course, no one will agree with everyone 100 percent, but what is the mark you are leaving on the world? When the dust settles, is there anyone who can say that you care about someone other than yourself? I know we are predisposed to be our best selves when it will profit us in some way, at work or perhaps around certain family members, but how do you treat people who can in no way benefit you? How often do you go out of your way to assist others? There will be times that people will need your help, and more often than not, it will be at a time that is not convenient for you. In fact, sometimes I think God loves it when we are inconvenienced. He takes those opportunities to fine-tune our character. Character is big!

Your character is who you are when you are not under the microscope. It's not the person who is serving at church or volunteering at their favorite charity. Character isn't even who you portray on social media. All of those things could make you appear to be greater, nicer, and perhaps more financially affluent than you really are, but character is who you really are when you get behind the façade. Who are you really, as a woman of God? Do you have some attributes that are unpleasing to God? Addictions that need to be put in check? How is your attitude? Are you critical of others?

Women are major offenders when it comes to judgement and critical scrutiny of other women. I am not picking on you;

in fact, I remember when God showed me this character flaw in myself, and it was no laughing matter. I was so insecure, and let me tell you, when the enemy knows you suffer from something, he will do everything in his power to keep you right there. If he knows you are sensitive about your weight, he may send someone to insult the way you look in an outfit. If he knows you are sensitive about your education, or your lack thereof, he will seek out opportunities to make you feel that you lack intellect. That is just the way the enemy works. He is smart. He knows that certain things bother you, so he will repeatedly put you in those situations until you figure out his tricks, and I was no different.

I was always very self-critical. There was a period of time that I seemed to always see the best in others but never myself. I unintentionally befriended people with the same insecurities as I had. Sure, they manifested in different ways, but they were insecure nonetheless and very critical of others. You know the kind that just talk about everybody? At one point, their criticism had gotten so out of hand that I became fearful of making a mistake. I mean any mistake. If I tripped or did anything that other people would deem insignificant, this group would talk about it for days. I hated it, and I noticed they didn't trust each other because they knew the same way my flaws were always on display, their flaws were on display as well. No one was safe. Every failure or humiliation was up for discussion, and the pressure became unbearable.

I had to do something because my hands weren't clean in this, either. I had laughed at jokes at others' expense. Listening to gossip about my so-called friends, I was not in a place where my character was pleasing to God, and He was quick to let me know that He disapproved. The Holy Spirit really began to convict me about allowing negativity to pass through my lips. He highlighted for me the moments when I had decided to take glory in someone's demise or embarrassment, and then He promptly reminded me that I was not only laughing at them, but I was laughing at Him. Dumbfounded, I realized that this was a serious defect in my character, and I needed to make some changes. I had no idea how I had become so insecure. But God reveals truth. He never allows behavior that grieves Him to go unaddressed, and so I had to face the type of person I was at the time.

You see, your character is your best testimony of what God has done in your life. Your character shows the world that God is real. When he is the focal point of every event in your life, God will reward you with the desires of your heart. But you must seek Him. Because of His love for you, He will not take you somewhere your character will not keep you. He can't! Your place of destiny would be more dangerous to you if you did not have the character necessary to sustain you there. You not only would be a danger to yourself but a danger to others if you are not a person of character. God can't afford to allow you into a place of leadership when you have holes in your character, primarily because there will be people looking at you and judging the church based on your behavior. Is it fair? No. But it is reality.

I believe that your character is the single largest component you bring to any relationship, save your heart for God. If your character needs an overhaul, then you need to address it before God brings you the relationship you desire. There are so many relationships that begin incorrectly because the people involved lack the character and wholeness required to sustain the relationship. Realize that God bringing you to a place of wholeness has everything to do with your decision to work on you first. Develop those traits, and God will elevate you to greater responsibilities. You can't expect God to bless you with a man who will have impeccable character when you have not done the work to develop it yourself.

In the Word of God, there are so many women of character, but inevitably whenever we talk singleness, one woman comes to mind immediately: Ruth! Have you heard her story? Of course you have. Ruth was the daughter-in-law to Naomi, and Naomi had two sons. In an unfortunate turn of events, Naomi lost her husband and her two sons, leaving Ruth and her sister-in-law, Orpah, to become widows. An old widow, with plenty of her good, old days behind her, Naomi decided to move. She needed to eat and, given all she had lost, she probably just needed a fresh start. So, she decided to leave her daughters-in-law and encouraged them to go another way, in hopes that they would have the opportunity to marry again. Of course, Orpah did not need much convincing—there is always one! She knew she was still young enough to remarry, and why should she cling to this old widow? So, she departed. But beautiful, vibrant Ruth stayed. She decided that she would be loyal to her mother-in-law and vowed to be near her until death.

It still baffles me that she was so at peace with the possibility of never marrying again. Without question, Ruth was an outstanding woman of character for honoring her commitments and sticking by her mother-in-law's side. She was a woman of integrity, but she was also a hard worker. Let's read in Ruth 2:1–2 (MSG): "One day Ruth, the Moabite foreigner, said to Naomi, 'I'm going to work; I'm going out to glean among the sheaves, following after some harvester who will treat me kindly.' Naomi said, 'Go ahead, dear daughter.'" Notice here that Ruth was a woman of service. She recognized a financial need for her and her mother-in-law, and she went to work to fill that need. At no time do we hear Ruth tell Naomi that she was looking to find a man to take care of her. There seems to be a common trend here—often in scripture, we see God honoring people with far more than they ever dreamed possible when their focus was in the correct place.

Of course, you know the rest of the story; as she gleans in the field, the Lord shows her favor and a man named Boaz notices her. He tells his servants to make provisions for her, and because of his instructions, she is safe. He intentionally leaves her extra grain to gather. Nowhere in the story do we hear of Ruth quitting her job just because Boaz thought she was cute. I believe her work ethic was one of the most attractive things to him, and let me be clear before we continue: if you end up with a man who loves you and wants you to stay at home, good for you but do not think it will be easy. I guarantee you that stay-at-home mothers would tell you that a lot of hard work goes into running a household. Notice that Boaz made her work easier and more fruitful, but he never eliminated the work altogether.

This is where I think we get it wrong. We have this unrealistic vision of a modern-day Boaz seeing us serving and thinking that if we stop what we are doing and lay at his feet, he will eliminate work for us. That is not reality or the moral of the story. Boaz is meant to be an example of what God can do with someone who is faithful. Faithful to serve, faithful to their word and, yes, faithful to the work of their hands. Because Ruth was a woman of character, God led her to a man of character. If you want a beautiful life, you can absolutely have it, but there are no shortcuts in a life of purpose; it will require you to go the long way around and work for it yourself. As you work, God will see your hand to the plow and reward you accordingly.

Another problem that we, as women, tend to have is an inappropriate division of glory. We give relationships all of the glory and all of the honor and all of the praise (sounds like a song, doesn't it?). We see people getting married or falling in love, and we glorify their unions in our heads to a level that is virtually impossible to actually experience. But hear this: glory belongs to God and God alone. Your God requires that He be first; He needs to be your everything. I am a firm believer that a great deal of the reason we can't experience great relationships is because of our displaced glory. Sometimes we allow our own unrealistic timelines to erect these thrones in our lives, and we begin to worship at them without even realizing that we have removed God from His rightful place. However, His Word is clear. Matthew 6:33 (KJV) says, "But seek ye first the kingdom of God, and his righteousness; and all these things shall be added unto you." That means there is no time in this or any other season that we get to put anything before GOD.

When we idolize the idea of relationships, we forget that God should be the one pointing us to the one He has for us. So now, while God has your attention, you have plenty of work to do; focus on building yourself into the person you are attracted to. Do a wish list and cross-reference your life to ensure that you are hitting all of the areas that you desire for God to bless your man of God in, and as you turn that camera on yourself, you will soon see every area that God wants to improve for His glory.

Compromise

When discussing the kind of woman we want to become, we can't help but do an internal checklist of different areas that we want to improve in. I think that is wonderful, and I think you would agree that God is pleased when we are able to do self-assessments and correct bad behavior. It shows that we are growing in the ways of God. It also shows that our heart is pointed to Him and we are more concerned about His view of us rather than the world's opinion of us.

Good for you! But there is something I want to address with you as we begin to excavate deeper. I want to ask you a question: are you willing to compromise? Immediately, about twenty of you answered an undeniable yes! You see, compromise has a dual meaning in relationships, One is often overlooked, while the other is glorified in relationship discussions. At first glance, you view compromise as meeting your partner halfway, coming to a consensus, and making decisions even if you don't always agree—and you are correct. When you consider how you treat other people and their likes and dislikes, compromise is a great thing, an honorable thing. But there are some things that should not be up for compromise. According to *Merriam-Webster*, compromise is an agreement or a settlement of a dispute that is reached by each side making concessions. This means that two sides may have opposing views, and in order to come to an agreement, they both have to lessen their position. Compromise is sometimes necessary to foster successful relationships.

However, I also want to talk about the other type of compromise. What I want to discuss is how we compromise our moral and spiritual beliefs in order to get some form of instant gratification. Listen, sin is tricky! Sometimes you know every misstep you have made and, in some cases, a conscious decision to sin, and then there is the gradual way we fall, one small compromise at a time. Songs of Solomon 2:15, ESV says: "Catch the foxes for us, the little foxes that spoil the vineyards, for our vineyards are in blossom." This means that if we can root out the small compromises we make in our daily lives, then escaping the enemy's traps for us will be much easier.

For example, if I told you that the answer to never-ending wealth was to rob one bank a year for the rest of your life, you would have a clear understanding that I was giving you bad advice. You would see a clear path to your demise. Theft equals jail time, and no one wants to go to prison. Yes, you want to be wealthy, but some of us are not willing to risk our freedom to have it. Well, the enemy knows that! He knows that you are too smart to be drawn in by tactics like that, so he sends small, seemingly insignificant compromises to see if he can catch you in a snare.

The first thing to know is you have an enemy, and he is seeking you out. First Peter 5:8 (ESV) says, "Be alert and of sober mind. Your enemy the devil prowls around like a roaring lion looking for someone to devour." Trust me, he is waiting for you, but he is not stupid. He is a worthy adversary. He studies you. He knows your weaknesses. He knows the areas you struggle in, and because of this, he doesn't always entice you with blatant attacks. If your desire to be loved is stronger than your desire to please God, he will find cunning ways to send love into your life.

Compromise does not look the way you think it should. Usually, the enemy starts by dulling the senses, hence making the sin more palatable. What is a great example of this? There is a show on television that I used to love! It is centered around drugs, sex, and corruption, and all of the things that make these shows entertaining. But let's look at it a little closer, shall we? We are to be on guard, protecting the gates—our ears, our eyes, and ultimately our spirit. As a single, you have to be careful what you allow to take residence in your mind. A mentor of mine said, "Starve what you want to die, and feed what you want to live." Isn't that accurate? That isn't some grand revelation; that is plain, old science. If you feed something, it will grow, and if you starve it, it will die.

It is a lot harder these days because television isn't what it used to be. We used to have programming that actually ended, thus giving our minds a break. I may be telling my age, but when I was a little girl, there was no such thing as 24/7 television. Now with streaming services and every other kind of technological advance, we are bombarded 24 hours a day with mindsets and ideologies that are contrary to the will of God. If you are not careful to balance what goes in, you won't be able to control what comes out. The more we watch programming clad with graphic sexual scenes and visuals of fornication, the easier it is to envision it in our own lives. We begin to rationalize that some sins are worse than others, and we actually begin to believe that our sin looks better than another's sin. But this duality can't continue. First John 2:15–16 (ESV) in God's Word says, "Do not love the world or the things in the world. If anyone loves the world, the love of the Father is not in him. For all that is in the world—the desires of the flesh and the desires of the eyes and pride in possessions—is not from the Father but is from the world." You have to draw a line and hear me when I say that I am not saying you have to live the life of a nun and never watch television again. What I am saying, however, is that you need to know your limits and tune your ear to the Holy Spirit to ensure that you know what you are watching is either helping you or grieving Him in this season in your life.

I used to have an affinity for reality television. It was such a guilty pleasure of mine, and I would just fawn over all of the women that were dressed to the nines with full studio makeup on just to go to Starbucks or the local grocery store. When I accepted my call into ministry, my palate changed. As I rushed to watch my normal shows, I felt this ever-so-gentle tug at my heart. No, not a heart attack. It was more like a weird feeling of discomfort, and it only happened when I watched certain things on television.

As I began to cut those things out of my programming, I felt closer to God. Not because I wasn't watching certain things on TV, but because I had grown to know His voice and respond. Again, this is my experience and I am merely sharing it with you, so you can ask the Holy Spirit if there is anything that He may be quietly discussing with you that you may be missing in the busyness of your day. Personally, I knew all about the seven deadly sins discussed in the Bible: lust, greed, gluttony, pride, sloth, wrath, and envy. So, while some of these things were the main theme of the programming I enjoyed, I did not understand why I was suddenly so uncomfortable watching. I mean, other people I knew who were devout Christians who loved the Lord and served Him were watching, and they were not at all affected. I have a tendency to be very critical of myself, so I would dismiss how I was feeling and go back to my shows.

Time and time again, the same feeling would occur, and one day in my study time, I read this: "So whoever knows the right thing to do and fails to do it, for him it is sin" (James 4:17, ESV). That scripture really messed me up because as I was pressing closer to God to know Him more, I was ignoring the voice of the Holy Spirit. You see, what may be a seed of sin in my life may be perfectly fine in yours because we do not have the same strengths or weaknesses. I found that the shows I was drawn to were the ones that fed the very sin that I was asking God to remove, thus making it harder to imagine my life without them.

Now when I am a married woman, that may change, and I may not have the same experience when I see certain things in film, but the difference is that as a married woman, I will have legal license to discuss them with my spouse in private fellowship. Ha ha, I am only partially joking. There are some things that God needs to rehab in your life before that man comes into it, and sometimes that means going cold turkey. For me, I do not watch movies with lots of references to sex because I can't have sex right now. If you have a drug problem, watching someone inhaling cocaine on a regular basis may not be the best thing for you to watch. If you have a drinking problem and you want to change your life, watching content with drinking and partying may not be helping you. Let's be clear. The enemy wants you in bondage and he wants to entice you, so he will try to get you however he can, even if it is by convincing you that you are not compromising your convictions when you know you are.

Ask the Holy Spirit what may be sin for you. Ask Him if there is anything present in your life that may appear minor to you but grievous to Him, and then take a moment and pray this prayer:

Holy Spirit, I welcome You into my life and ask You to show me all areas where I have allowed compromise to creep in. Lord, I want to know You not just as Savior but as Lord, and I ask You, Father, to remove any craving or enticement that would cause me to compromise the woman of God You have called me to be. I confess all sins and ask that I hear You clearly and You make me brave enough to obey. Thank You for all You have done and will do in and through me, in the precious blood of the risen Savior, Jesus. Amen.

Appearances

Sweetheart, you are beautiful and gifted, and I applaud you for all of your accomplishments, but I want to make sure you are not walking into dangerous situations. As a single woman, there are going to be times when people would love to make something appear in a way that is contrary to what is actually taking place. I want to give you the tools to ensure you do not put yourself in a position to have to protect your name or purity. Whether we want to or not, we have to be aware of how things appear to other people. With the rise of social media and so many supplemental ways to cheat, you have to keep your wits about you. You can't afford to be passive and hope that everyone you meet has the best intentions toward you. You can't control the actions or motives of others, but you can certainly control what you do and what you will participate in.

In your season of singleness, you are in a crucial place. Whether you wish to accept it or not, single women are naturally plagued with a little more scrutiny than married women are, and God forbid that you look halfway decent. Remember that your adversary wishes to destroy you, and because he will do anything to destroy what is going on in your life, you have to guard your reputation that much closer. To be fair, you can't control how people perceive you, feel about you, or how people speak about you. If people are insecure, they are not going to stop being insecure because you decided to come around. But you can control the situations that you place yourself in. As a single woman, you must be very careful that you are not drawn into a situation that can be made to look like something it isn't.

For example, when I am speaking somewhere, it is customary to be introduced to pastors of churches in the area if they are attending the event. Inevitably, there is almost always a woman standing there. By default, the host pastor introduces me to the person he wants me to meet. That may or may not be the woman. When they introduce me to him, I speak briefly and immediately introduce myself to the woman. I have a brief conversation with her and then resume the conversation with the gentleman. You may find that it is not his wife; it may be an assistant, but you should always err on the side of caution. As a rule, when a married man is standing with his wife and having a conversation, I always greet her first. This is purely out of respect for her position in their relationship.

Some people will not understand that, but I am telling you that as a single woman, it will save you a lot of misunderstanding. You have no business spending extensive amounts of time in conversation with a married man, especially if you do not have a relationship with his spouse. I am not saying that I do not have male friends. Quite the opposite. I have plenty of male friends that I was very close to prior to their marriages. But once they said, "I do," I made it my business to include their wives in our friendship. It is not because either of us couldn't be trusted. It is because the Word of God says in 1 Thessalonians 5:22 (ESV): "Abstain from all appearance of evil."

Preexisting relationships notwithstanding, I do not doubt that your intentions are pure, but the fact of the matter is that you do not know what that man has told his wife. They may have an agreement between the two of them that they will have no friends of the opposite sex that are unmarried and unacquainted with the other spouse. If that is the agreement and he sends you a friend request on your social media, and that is the only way you two correspond, then you have been put in a position to look like you are having a dishonest relationship with the married man. It is no secret to those who know me that I hate social media; I hate it because it is, in some cases, more hassle than it is worth. But as a rule, if a man sends me a friend request, I send one to his wife as well. If the man has a problem with that policy, I unfriend them both. Period.

You are the keeper of your heart, and you are the one who has to look out for you. Don't allow a man to pull you into a situation that you know is innocent but looks suspect to those without the full details. Trust me, I know you are a very interesting person, but it has to make you wonder, right? Why is he so concerned about having a relationship with ANYONE without his wife finding out?

Remember, your intentions may be pure, but his may not. Do not allow your good to be ill spoken of. Do not work with, speak to, or hang out with any man that wants your relationship to be a secret. You are not the other woman, and if someone finds out about your interaction and it even appears to be a secret, you are now placed in a position to have to defend yourself. Every man does not have your best interest at heart. If he is married, do not cultivate a relationship with him unless he is okay with his wife being aware.

The Other Woman

In 1850, Nathaniel Hawthorne wrote a book called *The Scarlet Letter*. In this book, he discusses an adulterous woman and how she is caught in the act and branded to wear an "A" on her clothing for the rest of her life. This is an age-old problem, for years, women have been dealing with other women who have intervened in their marriage, and since we are talking about your character, I thought it only fitting to discuss how you, as a Christian single, should address opportunities to commit adultery.

Right now, sexual immorality is at an all-time high, and it is important now more than ever to carry ourselves with integrity. Though the conversation is somewhat taboo, we said we were going to be real. So, let's talk about being the other woman. Speaking as a woman who has been the other woman before, I am saying to you, don't go there. In your defense, some of you are the other woman right now in your dating relationships and have no idea. But some of you do, and it does not change the fact that you are on the side. Let me help you. If a man is almost divorced, he is married; if he is separated, he is married. No matter what he tells you, and no matter what reason he gives, if he has no papers with a signature on the dotted line, then he is married, and you are setting yourself up for a lot of pain.

A friend and I got into a debate about the separated man. She said, "But if you didn't know all of the details, how can you be held responsible? Would God really punish you for what you don't know?" The short answer is yes and no. If you find out on Monday that your man (or who you thought was your man) is married and you don't break it off until Saturday, you are in the wrong. What was wrong with Monday or Tuesday? Why delay your obedience? You may not have known, but the moment you were made aware, you became responsible and accountable to God. It is often said that "delayed obedience is still disobedience", and if you do not act immediately, then you are signing up for some of the consequences that may come with it.

I do not tout my innocence. I have looked down the barrel of the adultery gun, and it is easy to fall into if you are not vigilant about the relationships you invest in. There are men in the church that have no desire to be faithful to the woman they are in covenant with and will do whatever they can to collect as many women as they can. If you happen to be one of those women, let me tell you this: he is not leaving his wife! If he does, guess what? You don't want him anyway. Trust me on this one. Even if you manage to get into a relationship with someone who is separated when you meet him, God views that man as a married man, and you are the woman at the well! John 4:15–18

(NIV) says: "The woman said to him, 'Sir, give me this water so that I won't get thirsty and have to keep coming here to draw water.' He told her, 'Go, call your husband and come back.' 'I have no husband,' she replied. Jesus said to her, 'You are right when you say you have no husband. The fact is, you have had five husbands, and the man you now have is not your husband. What you have just said is quite true.'"

Think about that. This woman was sitting there, thirsty, when Jesus came up to her, and He not only met her where she was, but He met her with truth. We can't be used by God if we can't be real. It does not matter how you became the other woman; if you ended up on the side, then you will have to reap what you sow like everyone else. What is funny to me is women, including yours truly, who will be in a relationship with someone who was unfaithful to their spouse, and then when they are the spouse, they are completely shocked that the man isn't faithful to them. Listen, if you believe this is possible, then you have purchased a first-class ticket to Stupidville.

Don't be ashamed, as I was there as well. But hear me—that way of thinking is just asinine. He is who he is, and it does not matter who he is with; if he is a man who will cheat *with* you, he will cheat *on* you. I can't begin to tell you the humiliation that is attached to being in that position, and trust me, the Word of God tells you that you reap what you sow, and this is no different. I truly believe that every bit of heartache I experienced was because of the way we got together.

The deeper issue is if you are willing to accept that type of relationship, it screams deficiency in your own personality. There is something lacking in you that you would be willing to accept a half relationship instead of fully investing yourself in something whole. You have to ask yourself what need it serves. To be sure, there are many reasons why women will accept a relationship like this, but I believe a major reason is their inability or lack of interest in making the sacrifices that a wife must make. A wife must see him at his worst, and she has to love him anyway. She is there in plenty and in want; we know the vows. Conversely, the other woman has no ties to him or any of his problems. For every woman that falls in love with a married man, there are at least two that are praying that he never leaves his wife. She doesn't want the man; she wants the distraction.

But let's look at the root of this and call it out for what it really is. For whatever reason, she is broken, and this type of relationship absolves her from ever having to make a real commitment and thus shields her from ever being vulnerable enough to be hurt. But, sis, this is no way to live. God is clear on the situation—if a man is married, he is not yours. So, if you are entertaining a married man on any level, you are sinning against God. Yes, that means even text messages back and forth. Yes, that means emotional affairs. If you are doing any of these things, then you are indulging in adulterous behavior, whether you know it or not.

I am trying to help you, love. You are in charge of your relationship with God, and there can be nothing between Him and you, not even a man. God will not bless a mess. You can't steal blessings from Him, and you certainly can't take something from His hand and then hope He will transform it into something pleasing to Him. Trust me, on the off chance that God allows you to have what you think you want, the suffering you will endure will far outweigh any temporary pleasure you think you are experiencing. It is not worth it. Make no mistake, the same way you are using that man as a distraction for you, he is using you too in the same manner. When he is with you, he can escape reality and live in a dreamland, with no bills, issues, or anything that everyday life brings. For all intents and purposes, you are an amusement park. You need to decide how long you are going to allow yourself to be used this way.

God has something real for you. Absent of lies and deceit. A pure love ordained by Him. But He can't give it to you until you are whole. When you seek God and are honest with Him about how you feel, He will speak to you, and He will heal what ails you. This type of relationship is beneath you, and it does not matter what your motives are. You deserve so much more. So, end this type of relationship now so God can get glory from your life.

Let's Pray

Heavenly Father, change our minds. Help us to not be so limited in our thinking that we only consider ourselves. Help us to want You so purely that there is no room for this type of twisted relationship. Change our perspective. Help us to know that we deserve to be a helper the man You have ordained for us, not a form of entertainment for a man looking to be distracted.

Lord, we know this is not what You intended for us. Help us to spend not one more moment tolerating any kind of sin in our lives, and restore us, God. Restore our minds to want only what You want for us. We thank You for the cleansing and purging us now. And we thank You for breaking all ungodly soul ties. In the precious name of Jesus, we receive Your freedom, power, and righteousness. Amen.

CHAPTER

YOUR EXPECTATIONS

The desire of the righteous ends only in good; the expectation of the wicked in wrath.

Proverbs 11:23 (ESV)

Do You Have Standards?

First, let me tell you that having standards is not a bad thing. Having them may keep you single a little longer, but that isn't necessarily a bad thing, either. In fact, I believe that the fact that you have standards is commendable in this season where people are obsessed with the instant. These days, we are so used to having everything right now that women tend to settle for anyone for the sake of not being alone. This is a mistake! You are a child of the King. You really need to soak that in—royalty can only marry royalty for a reason. In times past, if a man wanted to marry someone of royal blood, the king checked his pedigree to ensure that the person requesting his daughter's hand in marriage wasn't a commoner. I know that sounds brutal—and in fairy-tale land, we are always so enamored with the idea that love conquers all—but please wake up! In order to dream, you must sleep and the last thing you need to be while you are allowing yourself to be found by a mate is asleep at the wheel.

You are not lying in wait. You should be spending the time in your hidden season wisely and asking God what He wants to bring into your life. It is entirely possible that you have no idea what the correct standard in your relationships should be because you have not bothered to ask for God's opinion. Sometimes we want something so bad that we don't even ask God if He is pleased, and then we invite Him in later to fix the mess we have made. Bad move! God wants to place in you the confidence to know when the correct man has found you, and that will come in this time you are spending alone with Him, but only if you ask Him.

This is a great time to remind you that God has not forgotten you. He is so excited about His purpose for you, and He guarantees that He will never change His mind about you. Romans 11:29 (NIV) reminds us, "For God's gifts and his call are irrevocable." This means that He not only knows what He wants to do in you, but He knows what gifts He has placed inside of you to fulfill that purpose, and He promises that He will not take them away. Knowing this should make you feel seen by God and all the more excited to press in to Him and ask Him what He has for you to do in your hidden season.

While He has you, ask Him every question you could possibly come up with as it relates to the man you desire to marry. You should also ask Him why you desire to marry. Don't misunderstand me—marriage is a beautiful thing when it is done with the correct person, but it can also be hell if you choose unwisely. Your standards are going to dictate what comes into your life. If you come across as someone who will just accept anything, then anything will come to find you. It wasn't until I began to truly seek after God that I realized that the absence of standards is how I ended up in my failed relationships. So what standards are you setting? Well, let's start by looking at Mr. Right versus Mr. Right with God.

Mr. Right Versus Mr. Right with God

How many times have we heard about waiting for Mr. Right? Do you know that the *Merriam-Webster* dictionary defines Mr. Right as "the man who would make the perfect husband"? Unsatisfied with this answer and, to be perfectly honest, shocked that it is in the dictionary at all, I looked up the word "perfect." That is when the ball dropped. In the *Oxford*

Living Dictionary Perfect is defined as: "a) having all the required or desirable elements, qualities, or characteristics; as good as it is possible to be; and b) absolute; complete." Do you see what I see? "Perfect" is an image we have built in our minds that lacks practicality. Nobody is perfect, Mr. Right is a made-up figment of our imagination. He is who we have been sold on television as the perfect guy, and we have praised him since birth.

Knowing this has changed my entire outlook on men in general. The world tells us that Mr. Right is tall, dark, and handsome. He has a great job and makes lots of money. He is an athletic bad boy and desires nothing more than to see you every day. He has flowers in his hands every time you meet and a smile that lights the room. He is chivalrous, a good cook, and faithful to the woman he loves. He has no problems of his own because he is so inundated with making things right for you that any of his personal problems merely fade away. He is perfect. He wants to raise his children, leaves the seat down, and is a sexual dynamo.

I am not saying that it is unrealistic for you to find a man who is faithful to you and a loving father. But consider just for a moment that we may have created this imaginary man in our heads, and we are worshipping this image so much that no mere mortal could begin to measure up to Mr. Right's standards. There was only one Superman, and he is in a comic book. Sure, he has been created to appear invincible, but when all is said and done, even he has flaws.

Think about all these fairy-tale relationships that are mentally forged by women every day and how devastating it must be to become wives only to realize that they eat, sleep, and make love to mere mortals! Mortals who are flawed, who don't always have the right answers or know the right thing to say. Imagine that! After all of these pictures and fantasies we play out in our heads, they have the nerve to just be... Men. Can you imagine the pressure it must be for them? They are walking into the situation behind the gun, and they don't even know it. That sounds like a long, thankless job! Can you imagine showing up for your first day at work and no one telling you what is expected of you, and then having your employers be constantly frustrated that you are not meeting their standards? That isn't a recipe for success; quite the contrary, if you were in that position, you would feel defeated every time you clocked in, and I imagine that men feel the same way.

Ladies, we have done a poor job of keeping our feet on the ground. We have gotten so carried away with society's idea of Mr. Right that we can't be objective anymore. These days some, not all of us, are even willing to go as far as lowering our personal moral standards just so we can have something that looks like what we might want. Once reality sets in, we realize something that may be very hard for some women to accept—there is no Mr. Right! The best you can do is hope to be found by Mr. Right with God, and even that is going to be a process. We are caught in a vicious cycle; we've gone from looking for Mr. Right to sleeping with Mr. Right Now, thus disqualifying us from Mr. Right with God.

Mr. Right Now is not who we want; he is who we settle for when we get tired of waiting on God. Trust me, ladies, I understand the struggle, but men sometimes get a bad rap. They tell the woman they are seeing, "I have no desire to be in a relationship," and the woman will say that she understands— but somewhere in her head, she heard, "I don't want to be in a relationship because I have not met someone as talented and beautiful as you." All of a sudden, she has resolved to show this man all of the reasons that she is perfect for him. But he told her from the beginning that he did not want to be serious.

Ladies, we must stop doing that; we have a bad habit of misinterpreting male behavior. When a man truly wants you, you will not wonder if he is interested in you or if he is wanting to take your relationship to the next level. But so often, we see something we want so badly that we will ignore what the man has already said. It may be hard to accept, but if he has been clear and told you that he is not ready and you stick around, then you have no right to be angry with him because you are at fault.

I am not talking about the man who is leading you on. If a man is stringing you along, the first thing you need to understand is that you are still in control of that situation. You have to ask yourself why you are allowing him to drag you through this faux relationship. You know that you want more than he can give, so why are you still trying to breathe life into a nonexistent relationship? Why are you allowing this man to lead you when he has articulated that he has no desire to be in this for the long term? You can't blame him, because you are the one allowing him access. Some men only see you as an opportunity and will string you along as long as you are willing to make yourself available. He has shown you who he is, and it is apparent that he is not interested in a relationship with you, so let it go. Saying what you want to hear should not be enough; you should be judging him by his actions. If he is telling you everything you want to hear but you see no action, at the very minimum, you know that he is selfish and focused solely on his needs, with no consideration for you. Either way, you need to let go so God can reveal you to the right man.

Allow God to keep you hidden and stop wasting time in relationships that are unfruitful in hopes that the right one will see you. What if he does? Is it fair to expect the right man to wait for you to finish playing around with the wrong guy? Think of it this way: let's say that you have a couple of things God wants to heal in your heart before your husband comes. By adding extra men to the equation, it is entirely possible that you are adding more hurt for God to heal.

You are to guard your heart, and you need to be able to discern between Mr. Right Now, and Mr. Right with God, but here is the key, you must be willing to wait alone. Being alone is not an indictment on you nor will it lessen your testimony; if anything, it will serve as a catalyst to propel you forward when you encounter the correct man of God.

Traits of Mr. Right with God

So, what do we do when we believe a gentleman that could be Mr. Right with God has come along? How do we recognize him? First and foremost, I want you to relax. In this time of waiting, you have been inclining your ear to hear God's voice. In your hidden season, you and God have had some heart-to-heart discussions about what you desire in your sent man, so now you have two things to do.

First, you have to trust God. He will not lead you into a situation that is not pleasing to Him. And second, you have to trust yourself and trust that you will hear Him clearly and act immediately. It is possible that you will go into a situation and think God's hand is in it and realize that you have made a mistake, but that is the beauty of this season. When you are committed to the Father, you are in constant communication with Him. He will not leave you in that situation if He is not pleased. Don't allow the fear of choosing another bad relationship keep you from having what God desires for you. You must have faith in your relationship with God and trust that He will help you when the time comes.

Now that we have gotten that out of the way, let's look for examples of a godly man, shall we? We can't begin to discuss a godly man without looking for a blueprint in the Word of God. Ephesians 5:1–2 (ESV) reads: "Therefore be imitators of God, as beloved children. And walk in love, as Christ loved us and gave himself up for us, a fragrant offering and sacrifice to God." When determining what you want in a man, ask yourself the following questions: Does he walk in love? Does he love his family and God's people? Is he compassionate, and does he look for opportunities to be a blessing to you and others? If you answered no, this man may not view his call to be a man of God at a level that would merit him being selected to lead you. I do not believe that every man has to be a pastor or preacher to be qualified as a man of God. However, I do believe that every man has a calling, and it is in his relationship with God that it is revealed.

Ephesians 5:3–4 (ESV) continues: "But sexual immorality and all impurity or covetousness must not even be named among you, as is proper among saints. Let there be no filthiness nor foolish talk nor crude joking, which are out of place, but instead let there be thanksgiving."

How is his conversation with you? Is it always PG? Or is he looking for every opportunity to insert some form of crude humor or sexual innuendo? If so, chances are that he has very little concern about your purity. He is most likely testing the waters to see how far he can go with you, even if just in conversation. On the other hand, if he is attempting to fully engage in sexual conversation with you, knowing that you are remaining pure until your marriage, at the very minimum, he is showing you that not only does he not respect you, but he does not value your personal convictions. He should care about you enough to keep locker-room talk (if he engages in it) in the locker room, because of the sacrifices you two are making in your relationship. Conversley, you should be asking yourself why a true man of God would feel so comfortable speaking to you in that way.

Ephesians 5:5–7 (ESV) says: "For you may be sure of this, that everyone who is sexually immoral or impure, or who is covetous (that is, an idolater), has no inheritance in the kingdom of Christ and God. Let no one deceive you with empty words, for because of these things the wrath of God comes upon the sons of disobedience. Therefore, do not become partners with them."

Believe it or not, someone who is asking you to give yourself to him when you belong to God is immoral. He does not respect your principles and is a greedy person. Only a greedy person wants what is not theirs, and until God delivers you to him, you do not belong to him. Your season of courtship is so important. When you are blessed to meet Mr. Right with God, your courtship will be equally important to him. He will want to show you that he can lead you in the ways of the Lord—and not just into his bed. I recognize that the world has made saving sex for marriage this big, ugly and impossible thing. We see sex everywhere. It seems we don't even value it anymore; but believe this, Mr. Right with God will wait for you. Not only because your purity is important to God but because he values his own purity and relationship with God as well. He sees the importance of patiently waiting to receive every blessing God has stored up for him. Even if it is you!

If we jump down to Ephesians 5:25–33 (ESV), God breaks it down even further:

Husbands, love your wives, as Christ loved the church and gave himself up for her, that he might sanctify her, having cleansed her by the washing of water with the word, so that he might present the church to himself in splendor, without spot or wrinkle or any such thing, that she might be holy and without blemish." In the same way husbands should love their wives as their own bodies. He who loves his wife loves himself. For no one ever hated his own flesh, but nourishes and cherishes it, just as Christ does the church, because we are members of his body. "Therefore, a man shall leave his father and mother and hold fast to his wife, and the two shall become one flesh." This mystery is profound, and I am saying that it refers to Christ and the church. However, let each one of you love his wife as himself, and let the wife see that she respects her husband.

There is so much goodness in this passage of scripture, but when the dust settles, it says Mr. Right with God loves his wife! Christ died for the church! He lived every day of His life in sacrifice for the church. And you, my beautiful one, deserve someone who will sacrifice for you. That means him leaving his mom and dad and shifting his focus to his family, providing, loving, and covering you. Mr. Right with God realizes that by loving you completely, he shows the world how much he loves himself. He understands that if he doesn't love himself, he can't begin to know how to love you.

Examples of Mr. Right with God in the Bible

Let's return to the love story of Ruth. Boaz is a great example of Mr. Right with God. He saw Ruth as she was working in the field. He had seen and heard the type of woman that she was. In Ruth 2:11–12, NIV it says, "But Boaz answered her, 'All that you have done for your mother-in-law since the death of your husband has been fully told to me, and how you left your father and mother and your native land and came to a people that you did not know before. May the Lord repay you for what you have done, and a full reward be given you by the Lord, the God of Israel, under whose wings you have come to take refuge!'"

Boaz saw Ruth working and recognized her work ethic, but he also checked her reputation. Because of what he had heard, he decided to grant her protection and provision. Boaz knew the possible danger she could fall into by hanging around the different fields, looking for scraps, and he immediately wanted to eliminate any factor of danger from around her. Could she have gone to another field? Sure, she could have. But he didn't want her to because there were dangers associated with doing so.

You see, the man that God has sent for you is concerned about your well-being. Please understand that you can absolutely walk this earth, never marry, and be just fine, but if God selects a man to walk into your life, then he should be able to assess when you are in danger; something inside him should naturally want to protect you from harm. Believe it or not, there are men out there that are so focused on what they want and expect that they are not focused on protecting you, when that is a very large component of his duty to his family.

Provision, provision, provision. Boaz saw a need and fulfilled it. I think we have gotten this concept mixed up in the twenty-first century. Now, if you and your spouse have a role reversal in your family and that works for you, then Godspeed. But I am talking about missing traits that should be present in any man desiring a wife. Every woman should want to bring something to the table, but please, ladies, ensure that he has a suitable table! Don't bring your diamonds, rubies, and dinner fit for a king to his molded, broken-down, and corroded picnic table. If he doesn't have a real job, bringing in a steady income on a regular basis, then he has a broken-down table. If he has mass amounts of children with different women, he has a broken-down table. If he has any number of children and is not paying a suitable amount of money to defray the expenses for their upbringing, that man has a broken-down table and more problems with God than you know. If he has never been able to consistently hold a job, has bad credit, and is content to leave it that way? Broken down! In debt? Broken down. You see where I am going?

Mr. Right with God is concerned about more than your beauty; he is concerned with the type of woman you are. Ruth put herself in a place to be found, and when the time was right, Mr. Right with God showed up and recognized her character, and God provided the favor. Ladies, you need to prepare yourselves to be the total package. I know there was a time when the perception was that we could get away with just exterior beauty, but those days are gone. Now don't get me wrong, there are men out there who just want a trophy wife, but I promise you, you do not want to be married to someone like that. You do not want to be with the man who sees you as something for display, because that man has no intention of being anything to you. His expectation will be that you will sit and look pretty when needed, and when he doesn't need that from you, he will put you right back up on the shelf until he has need of you again.

You do want a man who looks at you and is proud of you—but because he sees your true beauty from the inside out. You want a man so enamored with your character that it makes his desire for you insatiable. You want a man of character who can recognize the like in others. A man who sees all that God has placed inside of you and wants to accentuate those qualities. A man of purpose who will constantly be looking for ways to please God. And finally, a man who does not want to dim your light and is so secure in himself that he is not intimidated by your strengths but applauds and encourages them.

As their love story continued, there was a moment when Boaz and Ruth were speaking and he acknowledged that he was older than other men, and he commended her heart for him. He saw her as kind for choosing him, and because of her heart for him, he was willing to do whatever it took to be able to marry her.

Mr. Right with God will do what is necessary to have your hand. Let's not be foolish about it. Some of our expectations are just plain crazy. Ladies, you know we can require some ridiculous stuff. Ever met the women who have three or four children but don't want to date a man with kids? Or perhaps you have a girlfriend who is making an average salary but expects a man to buy her Louis Vuitton everything? What about the women who want their men to pay for million-dollar weddings when they know he only makes fifteen dollars an hour? I am not saying that a 10-carat diamond wouldn't be nice, but is it really a necessity? No. All of those things are nice-to-haves, not must-haves.

The man you are waiting for prioritizes the standard God has raised for us. If he isn't willing to hold up that standard, then he isn't the one. And who knows? You may get the man who can afford that 4,500 square-foot home after all. But let's not put the cart before the horse. There is a very big difference between a man being able to support and provide for you and a man having to acquiesce to your every financial whim.

Mr. Right with God Won't Care About Your Past

If you have a tattered past like most of us do, don't worry. God does not expect us to be squeaky clean; in fact, He sent His son for the most dirty, broken, and impossible circumstances you can imagine. He is a God of redemption, so there is nothing that you can do to pull yourself from the power of His love for you.

Romans 8:38–39 (ESV) says: "And I am convinced that nothing can ever separate us from God's love. Neither death nor life, neither angels nor demons, neither our fears for today nor our worries about tomorrow—not even the powers of hell can separate us from God's love. No power in the sky above or in the earth below—indeed, nothing in all creation will ever be able to separate us from the love of God that is revealed in Christ Jesus our Lord."

Ladies, there isn't a single thing you can do to distance yourself from the love of God. With repentance comes redemption, and God loved you enough to send you His very best in the person of Jesus Christ, and if He will send you His very best to save you, He will send you His very best to love and marry you. Don't allow the enemy to get in your head and convince you that you have made too many mistakes to receive the true blessing that God has for you.

I want to share a story about radical obedience. In the book of Hosea, God told Hosea to go and marry a woman. Not just any woman—a promiscuous woman named Gomer. This woman was a prostitute and everybody knew it, and he still married her, because with God, your past doesn't matter. Can you imagine what everyone around him was saying? They probably told him how ridiculous it was for him to marry her, ran down a complete workup of her past, and probably even named names, but Hosea followed God. In obedience, he married a woman who in those days would be viewed as dirty, but he saw her through God's eyes; he sanctified her, made her a wife, and had children with her.

You would think they lived happily ever after, right? I mean, here she was, adulterous and the least likely to be chosen by a man of honor, and God blessed her to find favor with a good man. But that is not the case. In fact, Gomer was up to her old tricks again. She was a wife and a mother, yet somehow got caught up in her past behaviors. So much so that her husband now not only had to find her, forgive her, and take her back, but he had to buy her back! His own wife! This was twice the Lord had shown her favor with a good man despite her past.

I am not telling you to go on tour and sow your wild oats, because every man wants a woman of virtue, but what I am telling you is that to the right man of God, God's stamp of approval is all he will need. Since God has a purpose and plan for your life, He will exhaust all measures to get you to that purpose because His will, will ultimately be done. Again, please do not take this as license to misuse what God has given to you, but every time you get weary in the waiting, and every time the enemy tries to tell you that you have done too much in your life to deserve something real and pleasing to God, I invite you to think of this story. No matter what you have done, baby girl, you still deserve it. You deserve it if you are twenty, thirty, forty, or even sixty! It is never too late for God to show Himself strong.

Are You What You Expect?

In your hidden season, it is very important that you are managing your expectations. You may be expecting your Prince Charming to have it all—a career, a beautiful home, no children, and A1 credit. You may expect for him to wear nothing but Tom Ford and, of course, take you out to dinner at a four-star restaurant every week. That sounds heavenly, doesn't it? There is nothing better than being loved by a man who smells good, can hang a good suit, and support himself financially. I am definitely not saying that any woman would disagree with you, but I do think that any woman of substance would agree with me when I say that you may again be confusing nice-to-haves with must-haves.

A great way of determining whether you are being a little shallow in your requests is to ask yourself if you are able to furnish for your future spouse all of the things that you would expect him to furnish for you. If you are expecting that your spouse will purchase you a brand-new home and you yourself can't afford to maintain a studio apartment on your own then, yes, you may be a little shallow and unrealistic.

I completely understand why this is a struggle. We have been conditioned to believe that we can sit back and wait to have everything done for us because according to the order that God has set in place, the man is the provider. That is 100 percent true, the man is the provider. But I submit to you that the enemy has twisted that belief into the lie that we do not have to do anything to prepare for what God has for us. So many women are sitting around, waiting for a man of God to rescue them from their own lives. Nowhere in scripture does God reference two Saviors. There is one Savior, and His name is Jesus. The moment that we accept that He is the only one who can save us, we take the pressure off of the prospective man that God wants to send, and we will be liberated to enjoy our relationship free of unreasonable expectations.

Do not fault yourself for falling into this trap. My expectations were just as unrealistic. After my divorce, I felt like God owed me a man that was a certain caliber. I felt that because I compromised and took what was in front of me, he owed me somebody fine! I mean, gorgeous! I had a whole list of everything I wanted him to be and I can laugh about it now, but the truth is that my way of thinking was no laughing matter.

Let's look at my wish list before I entered Foolery Anonymous, shall we? I didn't want anyone unattractive, short, or with ugly teeth. He could not have gray hair in odd places (i.e., his eyebrows). He could not be crazy (I think we all would agree this is fair), morbidly obese, or super skinny. He had to have a keen personal style (i.e., he would never dream of wearing a straw hat, floral shirt, shorts, and dress shoes together). He had to have impeccable hygiene (which is still a deal breaker). He could not have gold teeth or extreme gaps between each tooth. And the list goes on. I had a distinct idea of what I thought was acceptable. I had a very particular man that I wanted God to bless me with, and so I was "waiting" until that man came along.

I remember a friend telling me that I was being very superficial. I was astounded. I could not believe that he said that to me. He explained that a lot of the things that I was viewing as unattractive were things that could be changed. For example, as single women, we are always hearing people tell us we have to look beyond looks and see straight into the heart in order to recognize the man that God has in store for us. I remember joking with someone and telling them that I had compromised in previous relationships and ended up with someone who still broke my heart, so I felt like God owed me someone that looked like a certain British African-American actor who shall remain nameless. I felt like I had already paid my debt to society, and this time I wanted someone tall, fine, and RICH!

As much as this was funny at the time, as time passed, I began to notice a trend. Nobody, I mean nobody, seemed to pass the test. It was never the perfect combination. No matter how eligible other people might have thought a man was for me, I found something to disqualify him. If he had a job, it was the wrong type. If he had a good job, he had horrible teeth, If he had great teeth, I hated his sense of style. If he had great style, he was too old or too young. You name it, if I could, I picked him apart.

Another issue that I think needs to be mentioned is that some of us have a tendency to date for our friends. We want to date men our friends would find attractive, and if he does not measure up, then we are on to the next guy. But our friends can be our undoing in so many ways. Some of your friends are miserable, yet they can see your situation so clearly, and they can't even commit to an outfit to wear. Use caution when you discuss a man with your friends. I am not saying that you should not get wise counsel, because sometimes our peers can see things that we can't, but don't allow their voices to overrule God's voice. Only you know what you are asking God for, and only God knows what will truly make you happy.

Have you noticed that we, as women of God, have all of these checklists? Checklists can cripple us if we are not careful. Who wouldn't want to build a man? It would be so much easier, wouldn't it? We could just add all of the personality traits that we wanted into the man that looked the way we wanted him to look, and life would be simple. But would it be fair? What if someone turned the mirror on you? If you aren't willing to consider whether you are all of the things you want in a mate, then you may be setting yourself up for a longer wait than anticipated.

What I am trying to do is give you a dose of reality. You can't walk into a relationship with a list of one-sided demands. If you desire something from your mate, then you need to be compatible, because they are probably going to want the same in you. Unfair and unrealistic expectations will keep you single because the man you finally end up with will quickly realize that he is the only one bringing something to the table. How hypocritical. Do your part to make yourself attractive in more ways than one. You need to evaluate your expectations. Is it God or is it you? Is it reasonable or are you reaching a little bit?

I had to remind myself that I could not relegate God to my mental picture of what "the one" looked like. You may be looking for a Wall Street stockbroker, and God may have a city garbage man laid up just for you! So be open-minded. Listen! I am in no way saying that you should not have standards. Quite the contrary. But believe me when I say that anyone God has purposed for you will speak comfort to every area of your life. In essence, it has less to do with the man that you are asking

God to send and more to do with whether or not you truly trust God.

I know what you are thinking: *Lisa, God is not the problem. I have a solid relationship with God.* Well then, I have great news for you! Jesus says in His Word in John 15:7 (NKJV) that if you abide in Him and His words abide in you, ask whatever you desire, and it will be done for you. So you can rest easy knowing that you have nothing to fear. Since you have open communication with your Father, you will be able to hear His voice clearly and make informed decisions from there. Knowing this should lighten your load and give you comfort that you can trust God with everything, even your expectations. Trust me, this was hard for me, but soon I realized I had to let go of my laundry list of expectations and allow God to just be God.

Another issue we must address is attraction. Listen, God knows what you want. I used to be petrified that God would send me a man that was unattractive. But, sis, it's the twenty-first century—times are hard in the dating world. Even unattractive men with horrible personalities are trying to take you through changes! I am joking, of course, but the struggle is real. I hear you asking yourself, *What if I end up with a man who looks like he could star in the next remake of* Night of the Living Dead? My friend, take a deep breath. That is not the God you serve. He knows the desires of your heart. He is not going to send you a man that you have no chemistry with; He just doesn't do that. And who knows, he may send someone who you wouldn't have normally gravitated to, and God may change your heart. If He does, you will see the man He desires for you with His eyes, and your eyes will be only for him. If he loves you the right way, he can have one eye and a kickstand, and you will be happy, trust me! While I can't promise you a British-actor type, what I can promise you is a God who is faithful to supply your needs.

Our God loves you so much that not only does He make you a promise, but He provides backup that you can stake your life on. Philippians 4:19 (KJV) says, "But my God shall supply all your needs according to his riches in glory by Christ Jesus." This promise is applicable to every area of your life. I can't reinforce enough that this is a journey, and it is all about your trust in God. If you trust Him, then you have to believe that He has His best laid up for you. Once you truly understand His heart for you, you will see that His love for you is so strong, and that understanding should extinguish any fears you may have about Him sending you a man you are not attracted to. Try not to overthink in this area. Take your time. Enjoy your singleness, and as God begins working on you, you will notice that some of the things that seemed imperative before are not as important to you now.

As you are hidden, I caution you to incline your ear to the Holy Spirit; He will guide you through this process. When He reveals something to you, do the radical thing and obey, quickly! I am trying to save you a boatload of the heartache I suffered. I knew my situation was a mess when I walked into it.

I was having sex outside of marriage and felt the Holy Spirit convicting me about it, but I did not listen and true to form, I did what some—not all—of us have a tendency to do. We try to dress things up to make it look like God's will. In my case, I attempted to marry the person that I was fornicating with in an attempt to conceal my sin. Then I had the nerve to be frustrated with God when it did not turn out the way I hoped it would.

Don't make this mistake, ladies. It is important to remember that you can't ask God for something and then attempt to steal it out of His hands. Have you heard the analogy, "Trying to fit a square peg into a round hole"? Well, that is what it looks like when you try to rectify your mess by forcing it into the will of God. Remember, you cannot make God accept what He has not sanctioned. But because of His grace and relentless love for you, He seeks out opportunities to give you the desires of your heart. So don't read this and become discouraged. Change what needs to be changed and watch God blow your mind.

In Jeremiah, Jesus, our sacrifice, gives us a sneak peek into the heart of God in a few words. Jeremiah 31:3 (NIV) says, "The LORD appeared to us in the past, saying: 'I have loved you with an everlasting love; I have drawn you with unfailing kindness.'" Through the completed work on the cross and because of His unending grace and mercy, God favors us. He loves us enough to give us the desires of our hearts, but only when they line up with His desire for our lives. Isn't that great news? This is why

151

we have to be checking in with Him constantly to see if the things that we desire are not only pleasing to Him but also realistic.

What is your type? Do you even know? Would you recognize it if you saw it? Women like men in all shapes and sizes. Tall, dark, thin, heavy, short, light hair, dark hair. You name it, they love it. But what is your type really? Some women only like the bad boys. I think that the girl who gravitates to the bad boy gets a bad rap and let me tell you why. It is unfair for people to believe that society can dictate everything but how you choose a mate or what you find attractive.

Look at the way the entertainment industry plays up sex to advance their brands. A while back, a certain clothing line wanted to revolutionize the way we saw jeans. They wanted us to view them as sexy, and so all of a sudden, we would see these women and men in scantily clad tops or no tops at all while wearing these jeans. Suddenly everyone was dashing out to get these jeans, but let's look at what was going on behind the scenes. Some of these men and women looked like they were in the gym twenty-four hours a day. They were ripped, and quiet as it is kept, we probably envied them and the sacrifices they made to look that way. But people know that the way they look is unattainable. Most models have been Photoshopped, and some of us have to accept that we are never going to be a size four, yet something in our heads says, "Go buy those jeans! You won't look like the models, but you will look close enough."

Now everyone is dashing out to get these designer jeans, not because the jeans do anything different from other jeans, but because of the way the jeans make them feel about themselves.

You have been conditioned, as we all have, to take cues from the media on what is or isn't trendy, cutting edge, sexy, innovative and, yes, even attractive. Look at the example of the modern-day hero that the media has used in the films we have today. These characters have ripped bodies, and they are gorgeous and highly complex. But notice that Hollywood always seems to make our modern-day hero flawed. These beautiful men are often fearless and strong yet deeply troubled and misunderstood. And, of course, what is a hero without his damsel in distress? So, yes, they will save the day, but at some point, they are going to have a love interest that can see past all of his indiscretions and insecurities and love his troubled behind just the way he is. We laugh with them, we cry with them, and we even root them on. And while all of that may be wonderful for a feature film, if you don't want a life of parenting a grown man through doing the work in his life, then you are in for a rude awakening.

Even on television, there is a famous show that highlights a woman who is passionately in love with the leader of the free world. In the course of their affair, they both sleep with a multitude of partners! They are corrupt and very complex characters, and the dramatic storylines will have you on the edge of your seat every time. But, do you want to live that way? No?

I didn't think so. Who wants a life full of drama? Of course no one would voluntarily sign up for that, but what I am trying to get you to see is that by accepting this into our minds, we indirectly develop a set of subpar beliefs of what we will and will not accept in our own lives. If these thoughts go unchecked, we will meander through our lives and end up in drama-filled relationships every time.

Earlier I mentioned reality television, people will go to the extreme to embarrass themselves on national television and it continues to baffle me. While I believe that a good deal of it is staged, they are still willing to look like a complete fool on television as long as someone is mentioning their name—a classic case of what I call Displaced Approval Syndrome. Displaced Approval Syndrome is when we are so obsessed with having external approval that we will leave key parts of our destinies in the hands of others. We are constantly subject to the thoughts and opinions of others in an attempt to be accepted.

Taking this back to your relationships, I believe that you may not truly know what you want because you have been conditioned to believe that what you think you want and actually want are the same thing. I will say it a different way. Because of the distorted ideologies that are constantly shoved down our throats by mainstream media, you truly believe that what you are attracted to and what you want are the same thing, but they are not. Now, I am not saying that everyone has to go out and find a man that looks like a one-eyed wombat and then marry him. What I am saying is I have seen a lot of happy couples in my time, and nine times out of ten, the mate I see them end up with looks nothing like they envisioned him to look. However, they are beyond content and genuinely happy because they ended up with everything they wanted, even if it was accidentally.

So, I'll ask again, do you even know what you want? Do you know how you want to feel? Do you know what you want to add to that person's life? My next statement is going to be somewhat controversial, but listen up, you should not be tasked with improving anyone's life. They should already have a great life. You should be the icing, not the whole dang cake! If all he is bringing to the table are eggs and a mixer, then guess what you have? Scrambled eggs! But if he is a diligent man of God, then his cake should be chilling on the cooling rack and he finds you to finish it off, so to speak. And don't think I am giving you a free pass to sit around waiting for someone with everything on the ball to come and pick you up! You better have some cake of your own!

I think that is by far the greatest misconception about relationships. There are three types of women. One prepares herself so that she has the richest icing available. Think about it. Sure, you can take about three ingredients and make a pretty lackluster icing. It's okay and it probably tastes good enough, but it is no cream-cheese icing, right? Cream-cheese icing is rich and decadent. You don't want to be meringue; you want to be

155

on par with a chocolate ganache or mousse, and that is a completely different level. Ladies, step your game up and become as rich (I am not talking about cash, but that helps too) as possible. Start your own business. Write that book. Make that music. Do whatever you feel the Lord leading you to do so that when you are found, the man who encounters you knows he is dealing with a woman of quality.

The second woman has her own cake and icing, therefore making the man feel expendable. If there is nothing a man can do for you, then your chances of encountering a real man are slim. I am not saying that you should not train to do things for yourself; I am saying once he is there, sit back and release him to be the man. If he likes taking the cars to the dealership, let him take them. But let him know that there is a place for him in your life. When I am out in the world, moving and shaking, I am a pit bull in a skirt. I can go from boardroom to cookout in a heartbeat, but when I come home, at the end of the day, I just want to be someone's woman, someone's good thing. You can't do that if you are so pro-feminism that you don't need a man anymore. Men are not the enemy. We are an awesome complement to them, as they should be for us. Can you make it in this life without one? Absolutely, but you need to ask yourself if you want to. If you do, then make that decision for your life, but don't walk through life blaming the absence of a good man as your reason for making the decision to stay single.

The last woman is willing to smear her icing on the table as long as she can say she has a man. What he has doesn't even matter; in her mind, times are hard! She has bought into the belief that men largely outnumber women, so she will not only take whatever she can get, but she will move heaven and hell to give him what he should already have himself. I am sorry, but there are women out here willing to be a mother, friend, and lover to grown men. Your man of God should be taking care of his business before you meet him. If he isn't, then when he gets to you, you won't have a man—you will have a grown child running around your house, having tantrums every time something doesn't turn out the way he wants it to.

Listen, if you are accepting a relationship with someone who has no intention of providing for himself, then you are doing yourself a disservice and greatly diminishing your worth. Let him put some skin in the game. Relationships are investments for both parties. If you find yourself in a situation where the only person sacrificing is you, then it may be time to reevaluate.

Let's Pray

Lord, we surrender our expectations to You. We want so much in this life, but more than anything, we want to be pleasing in Your sight. We abandon every sophomoric, immature belief, and we put on Your compassion and grace. Help us, Lord, to truly be who You have called us to be. Build us, Lord, so that we enter our relationships with our eyes and our hearts open. Do not allow us to miss our opportunities because we are so shallow that we can't move ahead.

Lord, You care about our hearts. Help us to listen and allow You to set the expectations in our lives. Lord, no timeline matters more than Yours. No desire overrules Your desire for us, and we yield to the leading of the Holy Spirit so say and do what You will in our lives. In Jesus's name. Amen!

CHAPTER 7

YOUR CHURCH

Disclaimer: My statements here are generalized based on my own experience at a particular church. These statements are not meant to depict the Baptist denomination in a negative light nor is this an opportunity for us to disagree about controversial issues that can only be resolved between you and the Lord. Because of the diverse opinions surrounding spiritual gifts in all denominations I invite you to seek God for the answers yourself.

Not forsaking the assembling of ourselves together,
as is the manner of some, but exhorting one another,
and so much the more as you see the Day
approaching.

Hebrews 10:25 (NKJV)

In this day and age, we are taught that we don't need anyone for anything. We are taught that we can be happy with Jesus alone. For most people, the church seems to be a place of comfort and refuge, free of ridicule and condemnation. Unfortunately, for some of us, it has been quite the opposite. Early in my upbringing, I can remember looking at church as something that we did on Sunday; it felt more like an obligation than a reward. My mother was the minister of music, so that meant that I lived in the church. Well, not really, but I might as well have. I felt like I was there 24/7!

What most people do not know is when you work for the church, you sometimes see far more than you would like to see. Some of the things I saw growing up made me question if there really was a God. I saw molestation, adultery, gossip, and judgement, and my mother was hurt time and time again by people claiming to love Jesus. Scandal after scandal plagued my upbringing. I saw pastors so in competition with each other that they weren't even concerned about how many souls were saved. It was a scary place to be and it taught me a lot, but perhaps not the correct things.

I was taught that if you tithed the correct amount of money, no indiscretion was off the table for you. (Please understand I am a tither. I am merely conveying that in my church, if you were a tither, you could get away with murder.) I just wanted no part of it. Church to me was a joke. Even now I cringe to think about the cesspool that some churches have become, and I am sure the devil is loving the division between us. We spend so much time segregated in our own little sects. It seems like church is about everything but what it should be about. We love to point the finger and have internal competitions about who is the most holy. Just consider that for a moment. Oh, how happy the enemy must be—he doesn't even have to cause division anymore. He can just sit back and watch the church destroy itself. We have become so preoccupied with fighting each other that the lost want nothing to do with us, and who could blame them? Where is that love for Jesus that everyone pretends to have? When I grew up, that love that I heard so much about was missing. Sure, there was a love of Jesus, but it was not demonstrated in an abundant life. Now please understand that I do not believe that every church is this way. In fact, I know they aren't but since the churches that are unethical get all of the press, it makes it harder for those of us that are trying to do this the right way.

My initial church experience was complicated. I have some great memories, but I also have some really bad ones. Understand that I was raised in a staunch Baptist church. There were no spiritual gifts to be discussed; in fact, at my church they were considered a thing of the past. My church only believed in preaching the plan of salvation, and that's it! No redemption. No real transformation. Just the same canned teaching for a solid eighteen years. I used to keep the youth in stitches imitating the sermons because I knew them by heart. It was funny at the time, but what was happening to me spiritually was no laughing matter.

At the age of eighteen, I made the decision to leave the church, and that is exactly what I did. I was done tolerating the façade and wanted no part of the hypocrisy. Please understand that this was before I was mature enough to separate God from the actions of His people. I had been hurt, I had seen too much and I wanted to try my hand at life without God. That is, until I had my first real encounter with the Holy Spirit.

My mother was a talented musician, and she would provide music to any church that called her, regardless of size or economic status and I hated it! However, it was an area where God truly gifted her. Years earlier, she had a stroke that left her vision so impaired that she could no longer operate a vehicle, and guess who became her driver? That's right! Me!

One evening, I drove her to this little church that had about ten human members and 100 mice! I may be exaggerating, but one Sunday there was one (literally) crawling up the curtain behind the pastor's head during the sermon. I almost passed out!

Depite my fear, that night, God sent a prophet to speak into my life. He was a portly Caucasian man with huge, windshield-size glasses on his face and greasy, stringy hair. He wasn't much to look at, and I can't even remember his name. He was one of those missionaries just passing through, but that man spoke more life into me in ten minutes than I had received in all of my years of attending church. I will not say what he said, but I will say that what he whispered in my ear that night was deeply personal, completely accurate, and life-changing.

That very night, I recommitted my life to God and got busy working and serving. For years, church was my everything. I served in three to four ministries at a time, but still something was off. I began to get overwhelmed and frustrated with the people of God. I am certain I am not the only one. I went through a very difficult time, and I turned to my church for assistance. I mean I was serving, so everyone should care, right? I was certain that in all my years of working, I would have forged at least one relationship with someone who would want to help me in my situation rather than discuss it, but no such luck. I was in the same place again: hurt, embarrassed, and now grief-stricken. I just couldn't deal, so I rebelled. My marriage was over, my mother was dead, and I felt like a failure. I felt so empty inside and I turned to the church for help, but they didn't seem to care. I became bitter, so bitter that I vowed never to step foot in another church.

After about three weeks, the Spirit of the Lord spoke to me and just flat-out asked, "When are you going back?"

My answer? "I'm not! I can fake all by myself. I don't need company for that, so why go and dwell with hypocrites? I am done."

The Holy Spirit compassionately asked me, "So, are you done with Me?"

"No," I replied. "Not you. Them."

He then said, "Then maybe you need to review why you are attending church. I never guaranteed that everyone you encountered on the inside of those walls would emulate My character. I did, however, call you to emulate My character."

That moment changed my view of church and my relationship with God as a whole. For years I was serving, but in service to man. I was showing up to be seen; I wanted people to know they could depend on me, but I got it all wrong. Matthew 6:33 (KJV) says, "But seek ye first the kingdom of God, and his righteousness; and all these things shall be added unto you." When I truly looked at this scripture a second time, with the scales off of my eyes, I realized that I had majored in the serving and minored in the seeking. I knew the call on my life, but I didn't know my Master's voice. I wasn't intentional about spending the time in Him and, as a result, I placed all of these requirements on the local church that really should have been just between God and me.

I often hear people say, "I don't go to church because some of those church people are worse than the people out here in the world." This justification is a very elementary way of looking at things. You see, if I go to work and everyone is late, it doesn't mean that I show up late, because I have made a commitment.

Don't get me wrong——given all of the recent issues the church has had to endure, I can see why it would be easier to just not be bothered.

However, at all levels of ministry, we need to be accountable to someone besides ourselves. It does not matter if you are hosting, leading worship, preaching, or even pastoring. You need to be covered, and before I throw a bunch of scripture at you, I want us to talk this through. Please understand that you need support. Every well needs to be refilled from time to time. There is no way you can walk through this life day after day, pouring yourself out to people, and never need your own soul to be replenished. That very need is what the church is for, walking in fellowship with others serves to advance us. Is it always easy? No. People can be fickle and very hard to deal with from time to time but having a support system is imperative in this season. Contrary to popular belief, we are better together. Ask yourself the following questions: What am I afraid of? Am I allowing past hurts to keep me from engaging with other believers? What do I need to surrender to God so that I can thrive in my service to Him and others? If God did not desire for us to attend the local church, then why does He ask us to? Is God the Lord over your life? How can you ignore that Jesus's primary trait was servanthood? Do you believe that you were called to serve others?

In my opinion, not attending church is a poor attempt at circumventing God's demand on your life. Our paramount responsibility should be serving people. We are to emulate His Son, and Jesus was a servant. He did not wait for the people to act the way they should act before He served. (Thank God He didn't.) He just served!

As a Christian single, you do not need a man who is saved but not serving. And beware of a man who does not feel he has to be accountable to anyone, because that accountability makes all the difference. Being saved is one thing. But an intentional relationship with God is another. Thriving in your singleness means that you are not satisfied with the surface of what God has for you. To be a real driven and successful woman of God in waiting requires that we go deeper. Servanthood is the deep end of the pool because it accessorizes your Christianity. On the other hand, serve people long enough, and it will break some things in you one way or another. Being next to other believers can sometimes show you things about your own character that you have never seen before, both positive and negative.

So often we read the scripture, "Not forsaking the assembling of ourselves together, as the manner of some is; but exhorting one another: and so much the more, as ye see the day approaching" (Hebrews 10:25, KJV), and because we have heard this verse over and over, we dismiss it as if it is insignificant. We ignore the preceding scriptures that substantiate why assembly is so important. We have diminished church down to a to-do list item. But if we read the text again, ladies, I promise you will see it differently.

> *Let's see how inventive we can be in encouraging love and helping out, not avoiding worshiping together as some do but spurring each other on, especially as we see the big day approaching. If we give up and turn our backs on all we've learned, all we've been given, all the truth we now know, we repudiate Christ's sacrifice and are left on our own to face the Judgment—and a mighty fierce judgment it will be! If the penalty for breaking the law of Moses is physical death, what do you think will happen if you turn on God's Son, spit on the sacrifice that made you whole, and insult this most gracious Spirit? This is no light matter. God has warned us that he'll hold us to account and make us pay. He was quite explicit: "Vengeance is mine, and I won't overlook a thing" and "God will judge his people." Nobody's getting by with anything, believe me.*

(Hebrews 10:24–31, MSG)

Do you see what I see? I see an opportunity. It is a privilege to worship God, to encourage other believers and tell them that God is with them. When I hear someone say they do not have to go to church to have a relationship with God, then I say that may be true, but how deep a relationship with God do you want?

Ladies, in your singleness, this is the time to prioritize service to your God so, yes, serve in your local church in obedience to Him. Let me say this again: your service in your local church is not about the people. It is about your obedience to God. If you approach your responsibilities with the understanding that you are serving God and not man, then you will be more fulfilled and lest apt to become weary. I know how hard it can be to sacrifice your time to serve while you are living your day-to-day life, but you can do it. God will be there to help you.

If you are gifted to be involved with a ministry that has ample work and very little resources, you may become overwhelmed. A few years back, I was serving in a ministry and at church six days out of the week. This commitment looked very good on the surface, and my pastors were very grateful, but inside I was a mess! I was uneasy, tired and, to be frank, over it. I felt like I had no more to give. When you arrive at that place, it is because you have not done a good job of stewarding your life. I am a living witness that I did not even know what balance was, and this is a hard place to be in when you are in ministry. You have to know that you are serving in all areas of your life effectively, and I wasn't. I had to take a step back and give myself some tough love. I wanted to quit! I told the Lord I just couldn't do it anymore.

Finally, in desperation, I poured out my heart to God. I remember telling Him how overwhelmed I was and asking Him to help me. He reminded me that He did not place those expectations on me, but I had taken on more than I needed to in fear of saying no. If you find yourself constantly overwhelmed and uneasy as you serve in your local church, it is possible that you may need to check and make sure that you have not put a yoke on yourself and called it God, for God's Word says that His yoke is easy and His burdens are light. Most times when we find ourselves frustrated in serving, it is because we have placed the pressure on ourselves, but God never intended for you to bear the load alone.

Another group of people who have opted out of church are those who have experienced what has been dubbed as "church hurt." Hear me when I say this: the church is filled with people. None of us are perfect, and we will all make mistakes. Unfortunately, sometimes it has been at the cost of others. Ephesians 6:12 (ESV) says: "For we do not wrestle against flesh and blood, but against the rulers, against the authorities, against the cosmic powers over this present darkness, against the spiritual forces of evil in the heavenly places." This battle that we are in is like any other war, and there will be casualties. Understand that the attitudes, cliques, and bad behaviors you may witness in the church are just by-products of the spiritual battles that are going on. It is not about you! It is about whatever spirit that person is dealing with.

I am not condoning this behavior; on the contrary, I am just trying to help you understand. For all of you who have been broken by the church, ridiculed, and told you weren't anointed or you didn't measure up, I am so sorry. Please hear my heart. I apologize on behalf of every leader, mean parishioner, or rogue usher that displayed conduct unbecoming of a child of the King! God never intended for you to be handled that way. He does love you, and remember, He never said that you would not endure suffering. In Romans 8:18 (KJV), He promises, "For I reckon that the sufferings of this present time are not worthy to be compared with the glory which shall be revealed in us."

All the hurt you have endured thus far will be far outweighed by the glory of God that will be revealed in your life. Don't turn your back on service to God because of hurt or an offense. God has great plans for you. Don't allow those who have given the church a black eye to turn you away from your purpose. No one in the church has it all together. We are a body of sick people, trying to get well. The difference between us and the world is that we know we need to be in the hospital. This is the season when you get to throw yourself wholeheartedly into ministry and focus on the things of God, so you need a covering. You need a local church. It is not a nice-to-have; it is a must-have.

Please know, though, that church attendance does not make a relationship. If you are just going to church and nothing about your life is changing, then you need to check your relationship with God and the diligence of your pastor. What is he feeding you? Are you ready for meat when he is still serving milk? Ask God where He wants you to be and serve there. Get planted, and no matter how uncomfortable it may become, don't leave there until He tells you that your time there is complete. Don't uproot yourself prematurely, and don't always look for a pastor that will only say what makes you feel good. If you know your life is clad with sin and you are attending church every Sunday and none of that sin is called into question, something is wrong. Every now and then, your pastor should challenge you. If that is not happening, I wonder if you are blooming where you are planted. If not, it may be time to make some adjustments.

Get involved in church, if for no other reason than because you want to be obedient to God. You will be surprised what He will do with you when you desire to please Him.

Let's Pray

Lord, we come to You now, asking You to restore in us the desire to not only attend a local church but to serve Your people. Father, we know that Jesus was a servant, and we want to emulate His character. None of our preexisting hang-ups will have power over us anymore because they are drowned in the blood of Your Son. Help us to seek You first, and we know all things will be added to us. Speak to us, Lord, and soften our hearts and spirits so that we can be a vessel for You, chosen and set apart. Root out our pain so that we can serve from a good place and, Lord, inspire us to serve more effectively. Help us to stop looking to people to provide what only You can. Heal our hearts and restore Your Church for Your glory. We want Your kingdom to come and Your will, not ours, to be done.

So today, we as women of God declare that we will build Your Church, not tear it down. We will not tear it down with gossip, and we will not tear it down with backbiting, negative behavior, or hatred. Instead, we vow to build Your Church in love and upon Your Son Jesus, who was the best representation of love. Help us to do better and be better. In Jesus's name, we pray. Amen.

CHAPTER 8

YOUR SELF-WORTH

I praise you because I am fearfully and wonderfully made; your works are wonderful, I know that full well.

Psalm 139:14 NIV

This is a sticky subject for me. I always thought very highly of myself, or so I thought I did. I never thought I would find myself in a position to have to teach myself how to love again, but I was there. I had somehow sunken into an abyss of doubt and low self-esteem, and I had no idea how I ended up there.

If I think back, I have to say that it began with the death of my mother. She raised me alone. She knew how harsh the world could be; she had suffered some pretty terrifying conditions and wanted to prepare me to face it, so she was always honest with me and intentional about pouring into me. She would tell me how beautiful I was and remind me that my size did not define me. I was always a plus-sized young lady; from the age of about seven, I took steroids to combat asthma, so naturally I gained lots of weight. You would think that would have had a really negative effect on me, but you couldn't tell me anything! I knew how beautiful I was. My mother made sure of it! My confidence was through the roof. She was the most important part of my life, and so much of who I thought I was had to do with her.

After my mother died, I found myself kind of mindlessly going through all of the motions when fear set in. I was terrified. I realized that my life would never be the same, and I did not know how to live in this world without her in it. I was lost. Every bit of normalcy was gone, and I was left with no one, just me, and who was that?

At the time, I couldn't even tell you; so much of my identity was wrapped up in who she was that I ceased to exist or be seen. I labored with not knowing my self-worth for such a long time, and somehow in the course of everyday life, I just stopped caring. I put my life on autopilot and made myself a very low priority. I kind of just checked out. I was figuring everything out, and nothing made any sense.

Let me take this time to tell you that if you are going through a transition in your life that is as stressful as dealing with the loss of a parent, may I suggest that you do not start anything new for a while? Spend time with God and allow Him to begin the healing process before you consider any relationship at any time, because when you are in the middle of something like that, you are coping and trying to numb the pain. And anything will do. Take it from me, I lost every bit of confidence I had.

Not knowing what to do next, I threw myself into church. I actually thought that if I focused on others and ignored the agonizing void within me, one day all of my pain would magically disappear. Not so! In fact, I was so needy that I was searching for anyone to fill in this blank space now created in my life. I spent hours and hours a day solidifying and reinforcing someone else's self-worth with no thought of how to cultivate my own. For me, anything was better than focusing on my issues. I thought I wanted to make sure all was well for all those I loved. In reality, I needed someone, so in the process, I gave a lot of myself to a lot of people who did not deserve it.

There is nothing wrong with being compassionate for others; that was Jesus's very nature. But you have to be careful to guard yourself against people that will use you. The enemy can see your insecurities a mile away, and you can become an easy target for misuse. Matthew 7:6 (NKJV) warns against this. It says, "Do not give what is holy to the dogs; nor cast your pearls before swine, lest they trample them under their feet, and turn and tear you in pieces." The problem with giving of yourself when you are not confident in your own self-worth is that you are giving something away that you, yourself, do not possess. The mere fact that you do not possess a high self-esteem makes you incapable of recognizing someone who will be a good steward over what you trust them with.

Please understand that I am by no means saying you should be selfish, but you should be giving to those worthy of the awesome gift that you are. The danger in giving to those unworthy of you is that if you are not watchful and aware; you will give and give until you have nothing left. All the while, you are hoping that someone will pour into you at the same level. You will develop a deep resentment and self-hatred because you somehow can muster up the courage to give care to others while knowing you can't extend that same compassion to yourself.

Before we discuss this any further, let's acknowledge that there is nothing wrong with being a giver! I love that I was born, bred, and raised to be a giver. However, the lesson I missed was that it is equally important to know who you are giving to and what they are willing to give in return.

My mother had many amazing qualities, but one thing I always struggled with was how she gave of herself; it was sometimes too much and too often, and she was never concerned about receiving. I don't regret it, though, because it was a life lesson even still. She taught me through the turmoil she experienced that if there is no balance, you open yourself up to being taken advantage of. While as Christians we are supposed to show the love of Christ, I do not believe we always apply this teaching correctly in our relationships. There is a way to tend to God's people and His Church without putting ourselves in emotional, spiritual, and financial peril.

How does this translate to relationships? I see women every day who will be chief, cook, and bottle-washer to a man who can't remember to pick them up from work. I have seen women go to the ends of the earth to defend men who don't plan to bring anything to the relationship, just for the sake of having someone. That is not a man problem or even a sensitivity problem. That is a self-worth problem. When you accept less than you want or settle for less in your relationships, you teach people that your well-being or happiness is not as important as theirs. After a while, they begin to believe you. They start to become less and less concerned about you in the relationship and become more and more focused on taking care of themselves.

I have a question. If you have a mate who is focused on taking care of themselves and you are focused on taking care of them, then who is taking care of you? If you are struggling with self-image issues, I want to challenge your relationship with God for a moment. How can you believe so vehemently that God loves you when you feel like you can't love yourself? It is impossible. You would be surprised how many women of faith think so lowly of themselves but being meek and being timid are not the same thing.

To refuse to love something that God has made is to tell God that He makes mistakes! Don't believe me? Let's look at Psalm 139:14 (ESV), which says, "I praise you, for I am fearfully and wonderfully made. Wonderful are your works; my soul knows it very well." We read this a lot, but look at the last bit: "my soul knows it very well." It means, Lord, I know that You made me, I am special, You knit me together in my mother's womb, and You know all about me.

If you believe the Word of God, then you also must acknowledge that doubting for one minute that you are made in the image of God lessens Him. Again, you are telling God that He is capable of making a mistake. You are no mistake, beautiful one. Even when you don't feel beautiful, and even if there are a million women walking this earth that you feel are better than you in whatever arena, know that God thinks you are perfect and if you trust Him, then you must trust Him in all things. Ask Him to restore your self-worth, and know that no one can give you your value or sense of meaning except God the Father. He has the power to restore everything that has been taken from you, and your worth is wholly founded in Him.

Don't be like me. I lost myself, and not having a clear view of who I was in Christ took me through bad relationships and bad friendships. I latched on to as many toxic people as I could. I was so self-destructive that I could not see God clearly.

Sometimes we get so focused on finding our happily-ever-after that we don't see things that are chipping away at who we are purposed to be. God is waiting to restore you—you simply have to ask. Ask Him to reveal areas of your life that may indicate that you are accepting treatment reflecting low self-worth, and once He shows it to you, ask Him for the bravery to face it head-on.

Let's Pray

Father, thank You for making me in Your image. I have allowed my experiences and failures to lessen my self-worth. I know that You knit me together in my mother's womb before the beginning of time, and You still have a purpose for me to fulfill. Lord, help me to refocus on my marriage to You in my singleness. Help me to embrace this time of quiet with You. Speak to me, Holy Spirit. I ask you right now to destroy and restore. Father, destroy any negative thoughts that I may have about my physical appearance. Destroy any insecurities I may have as a result of childhood or adult experiences that have allowed the enemy to paralyze me from doing what You have called me to do. Destroy any self-critical voices that may try to speak up when I am walking in Your path for me. Destroy any self-inflicted wounds I may have caused as a result of my lack of trust in You.

Oh, God, restore the joy of my salvation. Restore my soul and rejoice over me with singing. Restore my faith in the men of God and help me to recognize my sent man from the healed place that You have brought me to. Restore every dream that lies dormant because of my fear and insecurity, and finally restore in me a holy boldness to know that I can do all things through You who strengthens me. Help me to recognize my beauty. Not just the beauty I have on the outside, but the beauty you placed on the inside. Help me to embrace my unique character traits and help me to know that I am not only good enough, but that you are proud of me. I am your daughter and you love me, accept me and call me blessed. More than anything Father, help me to know that as I incline my ear to you, I can be trusted to recognize the relationship that You have ordained for me, and I can finally see myself through the eyes of Jesus. Amen.

CHAPTER

YOUR REVEAL

———⚬⚬———

*Now unto him that is able to keep you from falling,
and to present you faultless before the presence of
his glory with exceeding joy, To the only wise God
our Saviour, be glory and majesty, dominion and
power, both now and ever. Amen.*

Jude 24-25 (KJV)

I hope in this time together, you have been able to truly embrace who you really are. I know it is hard. We are always looking for others to define our beauty. What is it about women? We are just never satisfied. If we have straight hair, we want

181

curly hair. If we are thin, we want to be curvy. If we are curvy, we want to be thinner. We are just never quite content with who God made us. It is sad to see women who are constantly comparing themselves to other women.

But I know a secret: you are beautiful! Did you know that? You are made in the image and likeness of God. He has fashioned you to reflect everything that is beautiful about Him. Yes, you are beautiful, with your freckles and your gaps in your teeth, and with your thin lips and thick thighs. You are just who God created you to be. Every day, we as women are told what beautiful is, but what you have to remember is that no one person can define what makes you beautiful. You have the exact features that God wanted you to have, and although it may not look how someone else expects it to look, you are gorgeous in the eyes of God.

I know it is hard to hear that because you think that God has to love you because He has no choice, or your parents have to love you because they have no choice, but that isn't true. The truth is, God is the giver of all great gifts, and because the power to grant favor is in His hands, He is the only one that needs to see you as beautiful. There is no woman on the face of this earth who can't look outstanding. If you care about your appearance and take pride in how you look, God will do the rest.

I was not always considered the most beautiful person, even in my family. I was overweight. When I was growing up, it wasn't the way it is now where people are more accepting of the woman who isn't the perfect size six. In fact, when I was growing up, all I wanted to be was a size ten. Now I am a size ten and am still considered overweight. But what is different? What has changed? My perception of myself has changed. I take pride in my appearance, and I may take a little longer to get dressed, but in the end, it works out because the most important aspect of my stepping out is how I look to myself. I am not remotely worried about how other people perceive me; my confidence comes in when I can see myself and like what I see.

I didn't always feel that way. I was the girl plagued with a negative self-image because I was depending on people to further validate my beauty. When I lost weight, you would have thought it would have gotten better but, no, it actually got much worse. I just didn't know who I was. Because I didn't, I would focus on looking good on the outside, while I was shattered on the inside. I know how annoying it is to receive what I call "uncompliments." You know the ones I am referring to. When people say things like, "You are so pretty for a fat girl," or "You are really pretty to be a girl your size," or my personal favorite, "You must be very smart." Who said fat people were smart? Ha!

Anywho, I let those comments eat away at my spirit. Inside, I was so broken that I could not fathom that anyone could truly find me attractive. I was lost. I kept myself around people that would make me more insecure instead of having the confidence to remove myself from that circle of people. I am telling you this because you are more on the inside than you think, and when you really lay hold of that fact, your beauty on the outside will be undeniable. No one is attractive to everyone. Face it and accept it. But, there is someone who will look at you and be blown away by your beauty. Everyone else doesn't matter.

My favorite Psalm and the theme of this book is in Psalms 139:13–16 (ESV). It says, "For you formed my inward parts; you knitted me together in my mother's womb. I praise you, for I am fearfully and wonderfully made. Wonderful are your works; my soul knows it very well. My frame was not hidden from you, when I was being made in secret, intricately woven in the depths of the earth. Your eyes saw my unformed substance; in your book were written, every one of them, the days that were formed for me, when as yet there was none of them."

God made you just the way you should be. You are not ugly, and you are not old; you are everything you should be. You are not beautiful for a fat girl. You are just beautiful. You are gorgeous, and the things God will do in you are astounding. I need you to tell yourself that every day! Every day, you need to say, "I am beautiful, and the things God has planned for me are astounding. He called me; He formed me. I am made in the image and likeness of God. Therefore, I am more beautiful and more precious than rubies! I am a wonderful work of God's hands, and any man who has the pleasure of getting to know me would be favored by God." Now receive that truth and never forget it. It is your grand reveal, baby girl; you have labored and toiled. You have gone before the Lord and sought His face instead of His hand. I am so proud of you—you are well on your way.

I can't begin to tell you how proud I am to be a woman! I am beyond blown away by those of you who have chosen to champion your own lives and accomplish your goals. Gone are the days where we have to sit back and be seen and not heard. Now God has placed a demand on us, a holy boldness, and it is so good to see you all walking in the greatness that God has placed in you. When God made women, He made something special. Don't allow the enemy to make you feel like you have to be in constant competition with men! You are excellent at your role, and they can excel at theirs. We are in this together, so cheer them on as I cheer you on. Women are rising up to do great works for the Father. All over the world, women are embracing vision. We are positively affirming one another and cheering each other on. We are forward thinkers steeped in God's goodness. Meeting all over the world by way of small groups and vision-board parties, we meet not only to build each other up but to hold each other accountable to ensure that we are running with the vision that God has given us.

You are truly phenomenal. Contrary to popular belief, women have been doing it big for a long time. As a church girl, I was raised to believe that the ultimate phenomenal woman was measured by the woman mentioned in Proverbs 31. She was often the topic of conversation in my local church, and the epitome of a woman of God. Let's read a little about her.

A good woman is hard to find,
and worth far more than diamonds.
Her husband trusts her without reserve,
and never has reason to regret it.
Never spiteful, she treats him generously
all her life long.
She shops around for the best yarns and cottons,
and enjoys knitting and sewing.
She's like a trading ship that sails to faraway places
and brings back exotic surprises.
She's up before dawn, preparing breakfast
for her family and organizing her day.
She looks over a field and buys it,
then, with money she's put aside, plants a garden.
First thing in the morning, she dresses for work,
rolls up her sleeves, eager to get started.
She senses the worth of her work,
is in no hurry to call it quits for the day.
She's skilled in the crafts of home and hearth,
diligent in homemaking.
She's quick to assist anyone in need,
reaches out to help the poor.
She doesn't worry about her family when it snows;
their winter clothes are all mended and ready to
wear.
She makes her own clothing,
and dresses in colorful linens and silks.

Her husband is greatly respected
when he deliberates with the city fathers.
She designs gowns and sells them,
brings the sweaters she knits to the dress shops.
Her clothes are well-made and elegant,
and she always faces tomorrow with a smile.
When she speaks she has something worthwhile to
say,
and she always says it kindly.
She keeps an eye on everyone in her household,
and keeps them all busy and productive.
Her children respect and bless her;
her husband joins in with words of praise:
"Many women have done wonderful things,
but you've outclassed them all!"
Charm can mislead and beauty soon fades.
The woman to be admired and praised
is the woman who lives in the Fear-of-God.
Give her everything she deserves!
Festoon her life with praises!

(Proverbs 31:10–31, MSG)

To be honest, I wonder when the woman slept! She did everything! Her husband was happy, her children were happy, and of course her God was happy. She just had it together. Do you know how hard it was for me to latch onto the belief that being all of these things was even possible? Yet I see so many of you do it so effortlessly! You cook, clean, mend shirts, buy property, homeschool your kids, and look good at the same time. I mean, you do it all!

Women are in a different place now, but the mandate is still the same. We are movers and shakers, out here getting everything that God has for us. Our careers are thriving, and our family lives are booming. For those of us still waiting to be found by our knight in shining armor, it is easy to keep ourselves so busy that we do not stop to take the time to enjoy what God has done in our lives. We send up some token "Thank you, Jesus," and we move on with our day.

Our accomplishments hold little weight to us anymore. They don't even merit celebration; we are simply too busy! We are so consumed with getting that we are missing the best parts of our lives. We have to do better about celebrating others as well as celebrating ourselves. Don't be so driven that you can't sit down for a moment to enjoy where you are in your life. I know you have to get on to the next thing on your bucket list, but I am asking you—no, I am pleading with you—to slow down and take in the greatness that you are. You may have sold a house or written a book. Maybe you have graduated college or put children or even your own parents through college. Whatever it is, you are amazing! An outstanding woman of God! A force to be reckoned with! Don't dim your light so that others will not be intimidated by your success. They can do everything that you can do if they make the choice! But, they have to choose. Proudly accept all of your successes and, with humility, celebrate them.

You should be proud. You came out of the ashes. When people said you would be nothing, you chose to believe God, and look at you! Look at your house! Look at your children! Look at your life! It is a night-and-day difference from anything you imagined you would have, and here you are. After facing adversity, being shot down, and rejected, you still made it! Enjoy it! Embrace it! You have accomplished so much and should be celebrated accordingly. I am so proud of you!

Let's Pray

Lord, I thank You for my sister who is reading this prayer. I thank You that every one of her steps is ordered by You. Lord, I come to You asking, on behalf of my sister, that You would be with her through every high and low place. Help her to take her successes and celebrate them with grace and integrity. And in every failure, Lord, help her to know that You are there and her failure is temporary. Help her to know that You are ordaining her success, and because it comes from You, she must first acknowledge You. Help her to know that there is nothing wrong with enjoying the fruits of the works of her hands, because You said in Your Word that the blessing of the Lord makes rich, and You add no sorrow to it. So, Lord, now bind all worry—worry that she won't measure up, worry that she won't attain all she wants to attain, worry that she will somehow fall behind. Bind all spirits of busyness and fatigue, and allow her to bask in the light of Your grace.

Finally, Father, help her embrace the season that You have chosen to hide her and give her more of Your love than she has ever seen before. Lord, I speak vision into her. I speak a blessing on her business and her family. More than that, Lord, I ask that You awaken every dream that she has still inside her heart. Bring fire to her belly and joy to her spirit. She is Your child, and You love her so much. Help her to be the best version of herself yet.

Now unto Him who is able to do abundantly above all that we ask or think, according to the power that worketh in us. Unto Him be glory in the church by Christ Jesus throughout all ages, and the world without end. In Jesus's name. Amen.

REFERENCES

"6 Different Types of Abuse." 2017. REACH. March 23, 2017. https://reachma.org/6-different-types-abuse/.

"Dictionary by Merriam-Webster: America's Most-Trusted Online Dictionary." n.d. Merriam-Webster. https://www.merriam-webster.com/.

ESV Study Bible: English Standard Version. 2011. Wheaton, IL: Crossway Bibles.

Flammer, Josef, Katarzyna Konieczka, Rosa M. Bruno, Agostino Virdis, Andreas J. Flammer, and Stefano Taddei. 2013. "The Eye and the Heart." *European Heart Journal* 34 (17): 1270–78. https://doi.org/10.1093/eurheartj/eht023.

Holy Bible: King James Version Bible. 2016. Vereeniging, RSA: Christian Art Publishers.

Holy Bible: New Living Translation. 2013. Carol Stream, IL: Tyndale House Publishers.

Holy Bible: The New King James Version, Containing the Old and New Testaments. 1982. Nashville, TN: Thomas Nelson Bibles.

Peterson, Eugene H. 2004. *The Message.* Colorado Springs, CO: NavPress.

Siewert, Frances E. 1958. *The Amplified Bible.* Grand Rapids, MI: Zondervan.

The Holy Bible: New International Version. 2005. Grand Rapids, MI: Zondervan.

Vagianos, Alanna. 2017. "30 Numbers That Prove Domestic Violence Is An American Epidemic." The Huffington Post. TheHuffingtonPost.com. December 7, 2017. https://www.huffingtonpost.com/2014/10/23/domestic-violence-statistics_n_5959776.html.

ACKNOWLEDGMENTS

To my baby girl, my heart, my biggest supporter, and constant encourager, Taylor Brielle... You saved my life! In times when I wanted to give up, you have made this life worth living. You are the best part of me, and I praise God for the young lady that He is grooming you to be. I am constantly blown away by what He has given me in you, and I feel so very humbled to have been chosen to be your mom. I admire your fire, your spirit, and your love for Jesus and His people. Never stop dreaming and never water yourself down because others can't handle your awesomeness! Be unapologetically you! Mommy loves you and accepts you just as you are!

To my father... You gave me life, and I am eternally grateful for that. Thank you and I love you.

To my daddy, Clyde... You gave me love. I feel special because you chose to father me; you stepped in and filled every gap in my heart. There aren't enough words to thank you for all you have done and for all you have been. Thank you for encouraging me and always believing in my dreams. I will love you forever and pray I make you proud.

To my mommy... Heaven has the best! Twenty-seven years was not long enough, but I am grateful for every word spoken into my life and every second spent with you. You were not just a great mother but a great human being and friend. There aren't enough words in the English language to convey what's in my heart for you. I wish you enough.

To my Annie... I wish you could see me now. All of those talks when you thought I was ignoring you have paid off. I listened to you and heard every word. Thank you for my sisters, I count myself lucky to have been yours.

To Barbara "Mom" Allen... The warrior! You taught me how to fight! You picked right up where my mother left off, and I am so grateful to God for your gift of love. Thank you for sharing your family with me. I love you more than you know. As this book went to print, you left this earthly realm with all of its pain and suffering and entered heaven, where I believe my mother was waiting at the gate to thank you for all that you have done in my life. I thank you for every reprimand, wiped tear, and belly laugh. You fought cancer valiantly, and I am beyond proud of your strength.

To my sisters and brothers, Tracy, Courtney, Crystal, William Jr., and Sagel... When we are born we are given people to walk this life with, some people are not fortunate enough to always remain close, but I can say from my heart that I have a special relationship with each and every one of you and that is the providence of God. I love you and praise God for you every day. Thank you for every word of encouragement, harsh truth, and unconditional love for me and my baby. This is so much better because of you!

To the Allen, Hale, and Crayton clan... Thank you for sharing your mother with me. I love you all...

To the squad, my dearest friends...Milon, Jasmine, Tosha, Danielle, Corey, Nicole, and Latoya Thank you for believing in me. You ladies have never left my side, and I can't begin to thank you for all of your support and tissues for my tears. You are the kind of friends I prayed for. Thank you for accepting me and allowing me the space to become who I am today.

To my family: The Blocks, Taylors, Simmons, Grays and Kuykendalls—there are too many of y'all to name... You know I love and appreciate you with all of the amazing gifts and talents that you possess! Keep going! I consider it an honor to call you family!

Daven, Norman, Fred, Brian T. and Lo... my supporters, motivators, and constant encouragers... You believed in me and I thank you! Neither time nor distance changes anything in my heart for you. Each of you is so special in so many ways. Thank you. #myconfidants

To the Houses… Thank you for being true men and women of God. My life is so much better because you are in it. Thank you for loving me and my baby!

To David and Tracy Pugh… You two are relationship goals! Two imperfect people, dedicated to loving God first and then each other. Thank you for showing me what love looks like. You gave me hope!

To my nieces and nephews… Stay with God! He will never leave you! Auntie loves you!

If I have forgotten to name you, charge it to my head and never my heart. I share this accomplishment with you all.

ABOUT THE AUTHOR

Lisa Dannielle is an accomplished teacher, speaker, singer and songwriter. She is passionate about Christ, personal development, and business. Professionally, she is a marketing executive for a global engineering firm in Texas where she is raising a gorgeous and opinionated basketball playing teen. Her love for God and the advancement of his people are her driving force.

Forward all inquiries and prayer requests to:
lisa@lisadannielle.com

Social media
Instagram: lisadannielle
Twitter: lisa_dannielle
Facebook: Lisa Dannielle

41711345R00128

Made in the USA
Middletown, DE
13 April 2019